The Universe Has Your Back

Positive Thinking in the 21st Century

Matthew Polk

The Universe Has Your Back: Positive Thinking in the 21st Century

ISBN: 9798861026277

-Table of Contents-

Chapter 6: Navigating Challenges with Resilience

Chapter 7: Positive Relationships

Chapter 8: Goals, Dreams, and Manifestation

Chapter 9: Embracing Abundance and Gratitude

Chapter 10: Living a Positively Empowered Life

Starting The Journey

Welcome to "The Universe Has Your Back: Positive Thinking in the 21st Century." In a world that's constantly changing and filled with challenges, this book aims to be a beacon of hope and guidance. We will explore the profound impact that a positive mindset can have on our personal and professional well-being. We explore the science behind positivity, share inspiring stories, and provide practical strategies to help you harness the power of optimism in your daily life.

As the author, I embarked on this journey with a simple belief: that in a world where information moves at the speed of light and life can be overwhelmingly fast-paced, the principles of positive thinking are more vital than ever. This book is not just about positive affirmations but also about cultivating a resilient and empowered mindset to navigate the complexities of our times.

The Power of Positive Thinking in the 21st Century is not a one-size-fits-all solution but a map for you to discover your unique path to a more positive and fulfilling life. It's about finding hope, resilience, and joy even in the face of adversity. You will also find practical exercises, thought-provoking questions, and actionable steps to help you apply the principles of positivity in your daily routine.

I encourage you to approach this book with an open mind. Embrace the journey of self-discovery and personal growth that lies ahead. Whether you seek to overcome challenges, achieve your goals, or simply live a happier life, this book offers insights and tools to help you on your path. Thank you for picking up this book and embarking on this transformative journey with me. I hope it becomes a trusted companion on your quest for a brighter, more positive future.

"Your mind is a powerful generator of thoughts and beliefs, shaping your reality and influencing the universe. Embrace the limitless potential of positive thinking, and watch as the universe aligns to manifest your desires."

Chapter 1: Embracing Positive Thinking in The Modern World

1.1 The Important of Positive Thinking Today

In the fast-paced and interconnected world of the 21st century, our lives have been transformed in remarkable ways. We have access to an abundance of information at our fingertips, the ability to connect with people worldwide in an instant, and opportunities for personal and professional growth like never before. However, this modern lifestyle also comes with its unique set of challenges.

In this digital age, we are constantly bombarded with an overwhelming amount of information. The internet, social media, and 24/7 news cycles deliver an incessant stream of data, opinions, and updates. The sheer volume of information can lead to information overload, making it difficult to discern what is essential and what is noise. This overload can result in feelings of stress, anxiety, and mental fatigue as we struggle to keep up.

The current era has ushered in a host of changes in the way we live, work, and connect with one another. While these advancements have brought unprecedented opportunities, they have also introduced a unique set of challenges that individuals must navigate in their daily lives.

Many individuals today lead busy lives characterized by packed schedules. Balancing work, family commitments, personal projects, and social obligations often leaves little room for relaxation and self-care. The state of the world is marked by rapid technological advancements and global events that introduce a sense of uncertainty about the future. People often grapple with concerns about job security, economic stability, and the ever-evolving landscape of industries. The pace of change can create a sense of unease and apprehension about what lies ahead.

Achieving a healthy work-life balance has become another problem for many in the present-day. The boundaries between work and personal life can blur, leading to a constant state of connectivity and an inability to disconnect from work-related matters during leisure time.

This relentless pace of modern life can contribute to chronic stress and burnout, affecting both mental and physical health. Along with our busy schedules, The rise of social media platforms has fundamentally altered how we connect and communicate. While these platforms allow us to stay in touch with friends and family, they also create a culture of constant comparison. People curate and share the highlights of their lives online, creating an idealized version of reality.

This can lead to feelings of inadequacy and self-doubt as we compare our lives to the seemingly perfect lives of others. Another major challenge that we face in our current age is dealing with all the digital distractions. They have become an integral part of our daily lives, with numerous ways technology can divert our attention and interfere with our productivity and well-being.

These distractions include constant social media scrolling, notifications overload, multitasking, online shopping, mobile gaming, endless content consumption, and of course the fear of missing out which compels individuals to stay connected and up-to-date with the latest news, trends, and events, fearing that they will miss out on something important.

This fear can lead to compulsive checking of news websites, social media, and other sources of information.

The most notable distractions that seem to affect the most people appear to be the constant media scrolling and dealing with the associated notifications. The allure of social media platforms like Facebook, Instagram, Twitter, and TikTok is hard to resist.

People often find themselves scrolling through endless feeds of posts, photos, and videos, spending significant chunks of time without realizing it. This continuous scrolling can disrupt work or leisure activities, leading to decreased productivity.

The barrage of notifications from smartphones, tablets, and computers can be overwhelming. Email alerts, social media notifications, app updates, and messaging apps all vie for attention. These constant interruptions can fragment focus and make it challenging to concentrate on important tasks. Imagine dealing with all this noise while also attempting to multitask at work or at home.

While multitasking may seem like a way to get more done, it often leads to reduced efficiency and increased distraction. People might attempt to work on a task while simultaneously checking emails, responding to texts, and engaging in social media, resulting in subpar performance in all areas.

Some people can effectively limit their time spent on social media and avoid some of these challenges; however, they still fall prey to other online activities such as online shopping or binge-watching content on whichever platform they choose, and often more than one. The convenience of online shopping and browsing can quickly turn into a time-consuming distraction. People can get lost in online stores, browse through product listings, read reviews, and add items to their virtual shopping carts, all while neglecting important work or responsibilities.

Others over engage on streaming services, notably YouTube or any of the other various content platforms that offer an endless supply of videos, series, and documentaries. While entertainment is valuable, excessive consumption of content can lead to hours spent in front of screens, often late into the night, affecting sleep patterns.

These challenges, while characteristic of the modern era, can have significant repercussions on our mental and physical well-being. The high levels of stress associated with these challenges can lead to a range of health issues. In response to these challenges, the cultivation of a positive mindset and effective stress management strategies have become essential tools for not only surviving but thriving in the 21st-century lifestyle.

These increased stress levels can have profound effects on our mental and physical well-being. Stress is a natural response to demanding situations, but chronic stress, the kind that lingers over an extended period, can take a toll on our health. A more in-depth look at the mental health issues include anxiety and depression which affect our mood and overall mental health. Cognitive function can also be impaired such as memory, decision-making, and our ability to problem-solve.

Eventually, these stress levels can affect our ability to regulate emotions, making it challenging to cope with everyday activities. Becoming more positive-minded we can begin to experience emotional well-being by reducing symptoms of anxiety and depression. When individuals focus on positive thoughts, they can better manage stress and develop coping mechanisms that contribute to overall mental stability.

On a physiological level, the practice of positive thinking can influence the release of neurotransmitters and hormones associated with well-being. Dopamine, often referred to as the "feel-good" neurotransmitter, is released when we experience positive emotions. This not only enhances our mood but also boosts motivation and a sense of reward.

Physical health is also highly impacted which can contribute to high blood pressure, an increased risk of heart disease, and a weaker immune system, making us more susceptible to illnesses, digestive problems such as gastrointestinal issues and indigestion. These elevated levels of stress will also disrupt sleep patterns, leading to insomnia and reduced overall sleep quality.

It becomes clear that cultivating a positive mindset and effective stress management strategies are not just luxuries but necessities in our current time. This new mindset will serve as a powerful tool for navigating the complexities of modern life and enhancing both mental and physical health. It will also guide you in defeating negative thinking patterns that will ultimately lead you to genuine happiness and success in any pursuit of life.

1.2 The Promise of Positive Thinking

You might have often questioned if positive thinking can really work for you in your life, maybe you tried it for a while but the stressors and day-to-day difficulties had you second guessing the whole process. Maybe you attempted it but then slowly fell back into the same patterns of being overwhelmed, or maybe you know all about the awesome power of thinking positively and just want to possibly learn something you don't already know. Whatever your reason, The more consistently and frequently that you are able to maintain this state of mind, then I am here to tell you that it truly works.

Positive thinking holds the promise of profound transformation in our lives. It is not merely a rosy outlook but a powerful force that can shape our reality and influence the outcomes we experience. By adopting a positive mindset, individuals open the door to a host of benefits that extend across various aspects of life. This new outlook has the potential to catalyze vast change in several ways. Firstly, it alters our perspective on challenges and setbacks. Instead of viewing difficulties as insurmountable obstacles, individuals with a positive mindset tend to see them as opportunities for growth and learning.

This shift in perspective enables them to navigate life's ups and downs with resilience and optimism. Positive thinking also has a ripple effect on our relationships. When we approach interactions with a positive attitude, it invokes empathy, understanding, and effective communication. Strong communication is fundamental in maintaining existing relationships and forming new ones. This, in turn, can lead to more harmonious relationships with family, friends, and colleagues. We will discuss this further in chapter 7.

The incredible power of positive thinking extends to goal setting and achievement. Individuals who maintain a positive mindset are more likely to set ambitious goals, believe in their abilities, and persist in the face of challenges. They harness the power of visualization to see their desired outcomes clearly, thus increasing the likelihood of success.

Lastly, thinking in a more positive manner is not a mere ideology but a dynamic force that can reshape our lives. It empowers us to view challenges as opportunities, enhances mental health, triggers the release of mood-boosting chemicals, improves relationships, and fuels goal attainment. As we embark on a journey of exploring positive thinking in the modern era, these transformations are at the core of what awaits us. Below are three short examples of the dynamic power and change that this new mindset can have on your life if you begin to harness it.

Keep in mind that these are just three examples among the myriad individuals worldwide who have harnessed the transformative potential of this profound mental process.

Sarah's life had been marked by a series of challenges. She faced a difficult childhood, growing up in a low-income neighborhood with limited access to resources and opportunities. As she entered adulthood, she found herself in a cycle of self-doubt, low self-esteem, and constant financial struggles. It seemed as though the odds were stacked against her, and negative thoughts often dominated her mind.

However, Sarah decided to take control of her life by embracing positive thinking. She began by challenging her self-limiting beliefs and replacing them with empowering affirmations. Instead of dwelling on past hardships, she focused on her strengths and potential for growth. Sarah also adopted mindfulness practices to stay present and appreciate each moment.

Through consistent effort, Sarah's life started to transform. She pursued education and skill development, eventually landing a stable job. With a newfound sense of confidence, she set ambitious career goals and took steps to achieve them. Sarah's positive thinking not only improved her mental health but also empowered her to break the cycle of poverty that had persisted in her family for generations.

Today, Sarah serves as an inspiration to others, sharing her story of resilience and transformation. She demonstrates that with a positive mindset, determination, and a belief in one's abilities, even the most challenging circumstances can be overcome.

Sarah's journey is a perfect representation of the remarkable power of positive thinking. In the face of adversity, she dared to challenge her self-limiting beliefs and ushered in a new era of self-belief and resilience. By embracing the principles of mindfulness and the practice of affirmations, Sarah not only improved her mental well-being but also transcended the confines of her circumstances. Her transformation from a challenging childhood to a thriving adulthood serves as an inspiring example of how a positive mindset can break the cycle of adversity and set the stage for boundless opportunities. Sarah's story reminds us that with unwavering determination and a belief in our inherent potential, we have the capacity to overcome even the most daunting challenges life presents. Next we will look at John's condition.

John had been battling a chronic illness for several years. The constant pain, medical treatments, and limitations on his daily life had taken a toll on his mental and emotional well-being. He often found himself in a state of despair, questioning whether life would ever improve. John's journey toward positive thinking began when he encountered a support group for individuals facing similar health challenges.

In this group, he met people who had embraced positive thinking as a coping mechanism. They shared stories of how shifting their focus from illness to wellness had a profound impact on their healing journey. Inspired by these stories, John decided to finally adopt a positive mindset. He started by practicing gratitude for the aspects of his life that were not affected by the illness. He also engaged in visualization exercises, imagining a future where he was healthy and vibrant. Instead of dwelling on pain, he focused on activities that brought him joy and fulfillment.

Over time, John noticed significant improvements in his condition. His pain became more manageable, and his overall health improved. He continued to work closely with medical professionals, but his positive thinking played a crucial role in his healing process. John's story clearly illustrates the power of the mind-body connection and the incredible resilience we can attain. His journey illustrates that even in the face of chronic illness, positive thinking can be a powerful tool for healing and recovery.

In our final example of individuals who have overcome incredibly difficult situations that life tends to throw at us, we have Emma. Emma's life took an unexpected turn when she faced a profound personal tragedy. She lost her spouse in a tragic accident, leaving her devastated and grappling with overwhelming grief.

Emma's world had shattered, and she felt as though she would never find happiness or meaning in life again. In the depths of her sorrow, Emma found solace in the idea of positive thinking. She understood that she couldn't change the past, but she could shape her future. With determination, she embarked on a journey of healing through positive thinking.

Emma realized that positive thinking didn't mean ignoring or denying her grief. Instead, it meant acknowledging her pain and allowing herself to grieve without judgment. She sought support from a grief counselor who helped her navigate the complex emotions that arose. As time passed, Emma began to shift her perspective. Instead of dwelling on the loss, she focused on the love and beautiful memories she had shared with her spouse.

She chose to celebrate their life together rather than mourn the passing. Emma began to set positive intentions for her future. She envisioned a life filled with purpose, growth, and new opportunities. She started a gratitude journal, where she recorded even the smallest moments of joy and appreciation.

Taking care of her physical and emotional well-being became a priority. Emma engaged in regular exercise, ate healthily, and practiced mindfulness meditation. These self-care routines helped her regain a sense of balance and inner strength. Emma found meaning in giving back to her community. She volunteered at a local charity organization, offering her time and support to those in need. This act of kindness not only made a positive impact on others but also brought fulfillment and purpose into her life.

Eventually, Emma's positive thinking became a powerful tool for her healing journey. She learned to embrace life with renewed hope and resilience. While the pain of loss never completely vanished, it became a part of her story rather than the sole focus of her existence.

Emma's story also shows us the transformative power of positive thinking in the face of profound adversity. She not only survived her tragedy but also emerged stronger and more resilient. Her journey serves as an inspiration to others, illustrating that even in the darkest moments, a positive mindset can lead to healing, growth, and a renewed sense of purpose. Emma's life became a living example of the extraordinary potential of positive thinking to transform and rebuild after personal tragedy.

In the stories of Sarah, John, and Emma, we witness the extraordinary power of positive thinking to reshape lives in the face of adversity and challenge. These individuals embarked on unique journeys, each marked by their determination to embrace a positive mindset, and in doing so, they unlocked profound transformations.

Sarah's resilience against the odds, John's triumph over chronic illness, and Emma's recovery from personal tragedy stand as vivid examples of the unwavering strength we gain from this practice. Through the practice of positive thinking, they transitioned from states of self-doubt, pain, and despair to ones filled with hope, growth, and newfound purpose.

Positive thinking isn't a mere ideology; it is a dynamic force that influences our perspective on challenges, enhances mental well-being, creates emotional resilience, triggers the release of mood-boosting chemicals, improves relationships, and fuels goal attainment. These stories underscore that even when life presents its most formidable tests, a positive mindset can be the guiding light that leads to healing, growth, and the rediscovery of purpose.

As we navigate the complexities of the modern era, let these stories serve as a testament to the potential that resides within each of us. They remind us that with unwavering determination and the belief in the power of positive thinking, we can overcome life's most daunting obstacles, write new chapters in our stories, and create a brighter and more fulfilling future. In the embrace of positivity, there is the promise of transformation, resilience, and the renewal of the human spirit.

1.3 Your Positive Thinking Journey

In this section, we will explore the essential steps in embarking on your positive thinking journey. It's not just about understanding the concept but also about actively applying it to transform your life. Let's begin this journey together. Before we dive into the practical aspects of positive thinking, it's crucial to set clear intentions for what you hope to achieve with this book. Take a moment to reflect on your goals and aspirations.

What areas of your life do you wish to improve through positive thinking? Whether it's enhancing your mental well-being, achieving personal growth, or realizing your dreams, this book is designed to provide you with the tools and insights to make those intentions a reality. Positive thinking isn't just a passive concept; it's an active practice that requires commitment and dedication.

As you embark on this transformative journey, it's essential to prepare yourself mentally and emotionally. This journey begins with a clear sense of purpose and intention. Before we explore the practical techniques and strategies, it's essential to establish what you aim to achieve through the practice of positive thinking. Setting intentions not only provides direction but also imbues your journey with meaning and motivation. Here are some steps to help you set meaningful intentions:

Reflection of Goals: Take some time to reflect on your life goals and aspirations. What areas of your life do you feel could benefit from a more positive mindset? These could include aspects such as career advancement, personal relationships, mental well-being, or achieving specific dreams and ambitions.

Be Clear in Intent: Your intentions should be specific and clear. Rather than vague statements like "I want to be more positive," consider defining your intentions more precisely. For example, "I intend to cultivate a positive outlook in my professional life to improve my leadership skills and career growth."

Align with Values: Ensure that your intentions align with your core values and beliefs. When your goals resonate with your values, they become more compelling and meaningful. For instance, if you value kindness and empathy, your intention might be to use positive thinking to enhance your relationships and connections with others.

Visualize Your Success: Visualize the outcomes you hope to achieve through positive thinking. Imagine how your life will look and feel when you have successfully integrated positive thinking into your daily routine. Visualization can be a powerful tool for reinforcing your intentions.

Write It Down: Consider writing down your intentions in a journal or on a piece of paper. The act of putting your intentions in writing can make them feel more concrete and committed. It also serves as a reminder of your purpose on this positive thinking journey.

Set Attainable Goals: While it's important to dream big, also ensure that your intentions are realistic and achievable. Setting overly ambitious goals can lead to frustration and disappointment. Break down large goals into smaller, manageable steps.

Review and Adjust: Your intentions are not set in stone. Periodically review and adjust them as needed. Life circumstances and priorities may change, and it's essential to ensure that your intentions remain relevant to your current path.

Affirmations: Consider creating positive affirmations that align with your intentions. These affirmations can serve as daily reminders and mantras to reinforce your positive thinking goals. For example, if your intention is to boost self-confidence, your affirmation might be, "I am confident and capable."

By setting these clear and meaningful intentions for your positive thinking journey, you establish a road map for your personal growth and transformation. These intentions serve as guiding stars, helping you navigate challenges, stay motivated, and realize the full potential of positive thinking in your life. Remember that your intentions are a powerful force that can shape your reality, so choose them wisely and with a sense of purpose. Here are some key points to keep in mind:

Ability to Change: Positive thinking often involves challenging existing thought patterns and beliefs. Be open to the possibility of change and growth. Embrace the idea that your thoughts have the power to shape your reality.

Patience and Persistence: Transformations take time. Positive thinking is not a quick fix but a lifelong journey. Be patient with yourself as you navigate challenges, setbacks, and moments of doubt. Remember that persistence is key to lasting change.

Self-Compassion: Treat yourself with kindness and self-compassion. Understand that you may have moments of negativity or self-criticism. Instead of berating yourself for such moments, practice self-compassion and gently guide your thoughts back to a positive path.

Proper Mindset: Cultivate a growth mindset, which involves seeing challenges as opportunities for learning and growth. Embrace the idea that setbacks are not failures but valuable experiences that can lead to personal development.

Journaling: Consider starting a journal to document your positive thinking journey. Writing down your thoughts, experiences, and reflections can be a powerful way to track your progress, gain insights, and stay motivated.

As we proceed through this book, keep these steps in mind. Your positive thinking journey is not just about reading but about actively engaging with the material and applying it to your life. With the right intentions and a prepared mindset, you are ready to embark on a life-changing journey toward a more positive and fulfilling life.

Chapter 2: The Science of Positivity

2.1 The Psychology of Positive Thinking

The science behind cognitive psychology serves as a fundamental framework for comprehending the intricacies of positive thinking. It explores the various cognitive processes, mental patterns, and thought mechanisms that underpin our ability to adopt a positive mindset. Here, we can discover the multifaceted roles that cognitive psychology plays in our understanding of positive thinking.

This field of psychology helps us identify and dissect thought patterns and cognitive distortions that can hinder positive thinking. These distortions include catastrophizing, black-and-white thinking, and overgeneralization. By recognizing and challenging these distortions, individuals can reframe their thoughts in a more positive light.

Cognitive psychology explores the concepts of self-perception and self-efficacy—the belief in one's ability to achieve goals. Understanding how these aspects influence our thoughts and behaviors is crucial for positive thinking. Individuals with a high sense of self-efficacy are more likely to approach challenges with optimism, believing they have the capability to overcome them.

It also helps to shed light on automatic thoughts— rapid, uncontrolled, and often subconscious ideas that pop into our minds. These thoughts can be negative or positive. By becoming aware of automatic negative thoughts and learning to replace them with positive ones, individuals can reprogram their thinking patterns towards a more optimistic outlook.

This field of science also provides techniques for cognitive restructuring, a process that involves identifying and modifying negative thought patterns. This includes strategies such as cognitive reframing, where individuals learn to reinterpret situations in a more positive way. This approach empowers individuals to break free from pessimistic cycles and embrace a more positive perspective.

The study of optimism and resilience within cognitive psychology highlights how individuals can build psychological fortitude. Optimism, in particular, is linked to positive thinking as it involves the expectation of favorable outcomes. Cognitive psychology explores how individuals can generate optimism through cognitive strategies, enhancing their resilience in the face of adversity.

The science behind this also explores the power of visualization and mental imagery. By vividly visualizing positive outcomes and experiences, individuals can activate their cognitive processes to manifest these visions. This practice is closely aligned with positive thinking, as it encourages individuals to focus their thoughts on desired results.

Mindfulness practices, which involve being fully present in the moment, can help individuals steer their thoughts away from negativity and towards positivity.

Understanding the role of mindfulness in cognitive processes is integral to generate positive thinking.

Inevitably, cognitive psychology serves as a guiding light in our quest to understand and embrace positive thinking. It offers insights into the intricate web of thoughts, beliefs, and mental processes that influence our mindset. By harnessing the principles and techniques derived from cognitive psychology, individuals can navigate the terrain of their thoughts, overcome negative cognitive patterns, and cultivate a more positive, empowered, and optimistic approach to life.

Our thoughts have the power to effectively influence our emotions and behaviors both positively and negatively. Understanding the intricate relationship between thoughts, emotions, and behaviors is crucial in unraveling the dynamics of positive thinking. We will now cover the multifaceted roles that thoughts play in shaping our emotional experiences and behavioral responses.

One of the fundamental aspects of cognitive psychology is the exploration of the thought-emotion connection. It's well-established that our thoughts have a profound impact on our emotions. The thoughts we entertain—whether positive or negative—directly influence the emotional states we experience.

For instance, dwelling on negative thoughts can lead to feelings of sadness, anxiety, or anger, while focusing on positive thoughts can induce feelings of joy, contentment, and optimism. Recognizing this connection empowers individuals to harness the power of positive thinking to regulate their emotional responses.

Cognitive psychology introduces the concept of cognitive appraisal, which refers to how individuals interpret and evaluate situations based on their thoughts and beliefs. When faced with an event, individuals engage in cognitive appraisal, determining whether the event is seen as a threat, a challenge, or an opportunity. Positive thinking plays a pivotal role in cognitive appraisal by encouraging individuals to interpret events in a more constructive and optimistic light. This, in turn, can lead to more positive emotional responses and adaptive behaviors.

Exploring thought patterns further, cognitive psychology highlights how certain thought patterns can enhance emotional resilience. Resilience refers to the ability to bounce back from adversity and maintain emotional stability. Positive thinking helps individuals develop resilient thought patterns, such as seeing setbacks as opportunities for growth rather than insurmountable obstacles. These resilient thought patterns contribute to greater emotional fortitude in the face of life's challenges.

The link between thoughts and behaviors is a central focus of cognitive psychology. Positive thinking not only influences emotions but also drives behavioral activation. When individuals harbor positive thoughts, they are more likely to engage in proactive, goal-directed behaviors. This connection is evident in various aspects of life, from pursuing career aspirations to nurturing relationships. Positive thoughts act as catalysts for action, propelling individuals toward their desired outcomes.

This introduces the concept of self-fulfilling prophecies, where individuals' beliefs and expectations about a situation can influence the outcome. Positive thinking, when harnessed effectively, can create self-fulfilling prophecies of success and fulfillment. When individuals believe in their abilities and expect positive outcomes, they are more likely to engage in behaviors that lead to those outcomes.

Thoughts, emotions, and behaviors operate in a feedback loop. Positive thoughts generate positive emotions, which, in turn, influence positive behaviors. Likewise, positive behaviors can reinforce positive thoughts and emotions. This feedback loop highlights the dynamic nature of the thought-emotion-behavior cycle and underscores the importance of initiating positive change through thoughts.

The relationship between thoughts, emotions, and behaviors is intricate and profound. Cognitive psychology provides insights into how thoughts shape our emotional experiences and drive our behaviors. By understanding this connection, individuals can leverage the power of positive thinking to foster emotional well-being, resilience, proactive behaviors, and self-fulfilling prophecies of success. This knowledge empowers individuals to take an active role in shaping their thoughts, emotions, and behaviors to create a more positive and fulfilling life.

2.2 The Neuroscience of Positivity

This chapter explores the fascinating realm of neuroscience to uncover how the brain's plasticity, or its ability to change and adapt, is intricately linked to positive thinking. Understanding this connection offers profound insights into how our brains can be rewired to embrace optimism and cultivate a more positive mindset. At the heart of the neuroscience of positivity is the concept of neuroplasticity.

This remarkable quality of the brain allows it to rewire and reorganize itself in response to learning, experiences, and environmental factors. Neuroplasticity underscores the brain's inherent capacity for change and adaptation throughout life. Positive thinking is a potent catalyst for neuroplasticity. When individuals engage in positive thoughts and behaviors, they stimulate specific regions of the brain associated with reward, motivation, and emotional well-being.

These regions, such as the prefrontal cortex and limbic system, play a crucial role in shaping our thoughts and emotions. Thinking in this way leads to growth of neural pathways that reinforce optimistic thought patterns. As individuals consistently entertain positive thoughts and practice gratitude or mindfulness, these activities strengthen the neural connections associated with positivity. Over time, this process leads to the consolidation of positive thinking as a habit.

Neuroplasticity also allows for the rewiring of negative thought patterns. When individuals actively challenge and replace negative thoughts with positive ones, they initiate a process of neural remodeling. This reshaping of neural pathways reduces the dominance of pessimistic thinking and paves the way for a more positive mindset. These thoughts will have a direct impact on reducing stress levels, which is critical for overall brain health.

Chronic stress can impair the neuroplasticity of the brain and hinder cognitive flexibility—the brain's ability to adapt to new situations and perspectives. Positive thinking acts as a buffer against stress, allowing the brain to function optimally. The more individuals practice positive thinking, the more enduring its effects become. Neuroplasticity ensures that the brain retains these changes over time. This means that individuals can create a more positive mindset that persists, enhancing their overall well-being and resilience.

Understanding the neuroscience of positivity explains the brain's incredible capacity for change. It illustrates how positive thinking can reshape neural pathways, promote emotional well-being, reduce stress, and enhance cognitive flexibility. By harnessing the brain's plasticity, individuals can actively mold their thought patterns, creating a more positive and fulfilling life. This knowledge empowers us to leverage the brain's innate adaptability to embrace optimism and cultivate a mindset of positivity.

Now that we have a basic understanding of the neuroscience involved, let us venture further to uncover the key neurotransmitters and hormones that play pivotal roles in shaping positivity. Understanding how these neurochemicals operate provides valuable insights into the science behind a positive mindset. We will focus primarily on four *neurotransmitters* and two <u>hormones</u>.

Dopamine   Serotonin   Endorphins   GABA

<u>Cortisol</u>   <u>Oxytocin</u>

Probably the most widely known is dopamine, often referred to as the "feel-good" neurotransmitter. It plays a central role in the brain's reward system and is associated with feelings of pleasure and motivation. When individuals experience positive events or engage in activities that bring joy and satisfaction, the brain releases dopamine. This reinforces positive behaviors and encourages individuals to seek out similar experiences. Dopamine is a key player in the neural circuits that underlie optimism and positive thinking.

Serotonin is a neurotransmitter known for its influence on mood and emotional stability. Adequate serotonin levels are associated with feelings of well-being and contentment. Positive thinking is closely linked to serotonin production, as it promotes a positive mood and emotional balance. Low serotonin levels, on the other hand, are associated with conditions like depression and anxiety, highlighting the critical role of this neurotransmitter in generating positivity.

Endorphins are neurotransmitters that act as natural painkillers and mood enhancers. They are released during activities such as exercise, laughter, and acts of kindness. The "runner's high" experienced during physical activity is a result of endorphin release. Engaging in activities that trigger endorphin release can promote positive feelings and reduce stress, contributing to a more positive mindset.

Gamma-Aminobutyric Acid (GABA) is an inhibitory neurotransmitter that has a calming effect on the brain. It helps reduce anxiety and promotes relaxation. Positive thinking can enhance GABA activity, leading to reduced feelings of stress and anxiety. By creating a sense of calm and tranquility, GABA contributes to a positive emotional state. These four neurotransmitters can play a critical role in our pursuit for a more fulfilling and positive life.

While not typically associated with positivity, cortisol, the stress hormone, plays a crucial role in our understanding of positivity. Elevated cortisol levels are linked to stress, anxiety, and negative emotions. Positive thinking acts as a buffer against excessive cortisol production. By reducing stress and promoting relaxation, positive thinking helps regulate cortisol levels, contributing to emotional well-being.

Oxytocin is often referred to as the "love hormone" or "bonding hormone." It is released during social interactions, physical touch, and acts of affection. oxytocin promotes feelings of trust, empathy, and connection with others. Positive social interactions that release oxytocin contribute to a sense of positivity and well-being. Building and maintaining strong social connections are essential for creating more positivity through oxytocin release.

Understanding the role of neurotransmitters and hormones associated with positivity provides us with valuable insights into the physiological basis of a positive mindset. These neurochemicals influence our mood, emotions, and overall well-being, highlighting the profound impact of positivity on our brain's chemistry.

By actively engaging in activities and practices that promote the release of these neurochemicals, individuals can adopt a more positive and emotionally balanced life. This knowledge empowers us to leverage the brain's intricate chemistry to embrace optimism and cultivate a mindset of positivity.

2.3 The Feedback Loop of Positivity

In this subsection we discuss the fascinating concept of the feedback loop of positivity, which elucidates the interconnected relationship between positive thoughts and positive experiences. Understanding this feedback loop offers profound insights into how positivity can shape our lives.

Positive thoughts have a remarkable ability to shape our experiences. When individuals maintain a positive mindset, they are more likely to perceive and interpret events in a positive light. This cognitive filter allows them to focus on opportunities, solutions, and the silver linings within challenges. As a result, positive thoughts lead to a heightened awareness of positive experiences in daily life. These same thoughts act as cognitive primers, influencing our perception and attention.

When individuals harbor positive thoughts, their cognitive processes are primed to notice and amplify positive cues in their environment. This heightened sensitivity to positivity enhances their ability to extract joy, gratitude, and satisfaction from everyday moments. Thinking in this way will build emotional resilience and adaptive coping mechanisms. When individuals encounter adversity or setbacks, a positive mindset enables them to navigate these challenges with optimism.

Often they view setbacks as opportunities for growth and learning rather than insurmountable obstacles. This resilience, in turn, leads to a greater likelihood of positive outcomes. When individuals anticipate positive outcomes, they are more likely to engage in behaviors that lead to those outcomes. This expectation of success can influence their actions, decisions, and interactions, ultimately manifesting the positive outcomes they envisioned.

When individuals radiate positivity through their thoughts and behaviors, they influence the emotions and experiences of those around them. Positive emotions are known to be highly contagious, leading to more positive social interactions and creating a supportive and uplifting environment. The feedback loop of positivity contributes to an expansion of the positivity ratio in one's life.

By nurturing positive thoughts, individuals can tip the scales in favor of positivity, leading to a greater overall sense of well-being and life satisfaction. As positive thoughts lead to positive experiences, these experiences, in turn, reinforce positive thinking. This self-perpetuating cycle creates a momentum of positivity that becomes increasingly ingrained in one's mindset. Over time, positive thinking becomes a natural and habitual way of approaching life.

Understanding the feedback loop of positivity underscores the profound impact of our thoughts on our experiences. Positive thoughts not only enhance our perception of the world but also influence our responses to it. By actively cultivating positive thoughts, individuals can initiate a cycle of positivity that shapes their experiences, maintains resilience, and contributes to a more joyful and fulfilling life. This knowledge empowers us to harness the feedback loop of positivity to embrace optimism and cultivate a mindset of enduring positivity.

Breaking the Cycle of Negativity

Now we can dive into the idea of breaking free from the cycle of negativity and embracing positivity and personal growth. Understanding the steps and strategies involved in this process is key to maintaining a more optimistic and fulfilling life. The first step in breaking the cycle of negativity is self-awareness. Individuals must learn to recognize their negative thought patterns and automatic responses to challenging situations. Identifying these patterns allows individuals to take control of their thoughts and interrupt the cycle of negativity.

Negative thoughts often stem from deeply ingrained negative beliefs about oneself, the world, or the future. It's essential to challenge and reframe these beliefs. Cognitive restructuring techniques can be employed to replace negative beliefs with more positive and empowering ones. Self-compassion is a powerful antidote to self-criticism and negativity. Individuals must learn to treat themselves with kindness and understanding, especially during times of self-doubt or setbacks. Self-compassion creates emotional resilience and helps break the cycle of harsh self-judgment.

Mindfulness practices encourage individuals to be fully present in the moment without judgment. By practicing mindfulness, individuals can observe their thoughts and emotions objectively, detaching from negative thought patterns. This mindfulness allows for greater control over one's reactions and the ability to choose more positive responses. Cultivating gratitude is another powerful tool in shifting from negativity to positivity. Regularly practicing gratitude exercises can rewire the brain to focus on positive aspects of life.

Additionally, engaging in positivity exercises, such as affirmations and visualization, can help individuals develop a more optimistic mindset. Breaking the cycle of negativity often involves evaluating one's social environment. Surrounding oneself with positive and supportive individuals can provide an uplifting atmosphere that reinforces positive thinking. Healthy relationships and a positive social network contribute to personal growth. Positive thinking is closely linked to setting and achieving realistic goals. Breaking down much larger goals into smaller, achievable milestones allows individuals to track their progress and celebrate their successes. These celebrations reinforce positive thinking and further motivation leading to a cascading effect of success.

Persistence and patience are essential qualities to remember when it comes to breaking this cycle. It is important to acknowledge that setbacks may occur, but these setbacks do not negate the progress made. By persevering through challenges, individuals can continue to embrace positivity and personal growth.

The journey is ongoing. It involves a commitment to lifelong learning and personal development. Individuals can continue to explore new strategies, techniques, and perspectives to enhance their positive thinking and overall well-being.

Breaking the cycle of negativity is a profound and empowering journey toward embracing positivity, personal growth, and a more fulfilling life. By applying these steps and strategies, individuals can take control of their thoughts, cultivate a positive mindset, and embark on a path of lasting transformation. This knowledge empowers us to break free from the shackles of negativity and embrace a future filled with optimism and growth.

Chapter 3: Cultivating a Positive Mindset

3.1 Mindfulness for Positive Thinking

Mindfulness is a profound practice that lies at the heart of cultivating a positive mindset. It is a state of focused awareness and presence in the here and now. We can now explore the essence of mindfulness, its principles, and how it contributes to nurturing a positive and optimistic outlook on life.

Mindfulness involves the art of being fully present in the moment, without judgment or distraction. It is about observing your thoughts, emotions, bodily sensations, and the surrounding environment with an open and non-critical mind. Mindfulness allows you to become an impartial observer of your own inner experiences. This practice is guided by several key principles:

Awareness of the Present-Moment: Mindfulness directs your attention to the present moment, anchoring you in the here and now.

Becoming Non-Judgmental: A crucial aspect of mindfulness is suspending judgment. Rather than labeling thoughts or feelings as good or bad, you observe them neutrally.

Finding Acceptance: Mindfulness encourages acceptance of whatever arises in your awareness. This acceptance creates inner peace and reduces inner resistance.

Letting Go: You practice letting go of attachments to thoughts or emotions, allowing them to come and go like passing clouds.

One of the most common ways to cultivate mindfulness is through meditation. Mindfulness meditation involves setting aside dedicated time to sit quietly, focus on your breath, and observe your thoughts and sensations. This practice strengthens your mindfulness "muscle," enhancing your ability to stay present throughout the day. Mindfulness is not limited to formal meditation sessions. It extends to your daily life, transforming routine activities into opportunities for mindfulness.

Simple acts like eating, walking, or even washing dishes can become mindful practices. By bringing your full attention to these activities, you infuse them with a sense of purpose and presence. The practice of mindfulness yields a multitude of benefits for cultivating a positive mindset, including:

Reduced Stress: Mindfulness reduces the physiological and psychological effects of stress, promoting emotional well-being.

Enhanced Emotional Regulation: Mindfulness helps you become more attuned to your emotions and respond to them skillfully.

Improved Focus and Concentration: By training your mind to stay present, mindfulness enhances your ability to concentrate on tasks and goals.

Greater Resilience: Mindfulness leads to emotional resilience, allowing you to bounce back from setbacks with grace and optimism.

Increased Self-Awareness: Mindfulness deepens your understanding of yourself, your thought patterns, and your reactions, empowering you to make positive changes.

Enhanced Relationships: Being fully present in interactions with others improves the quality of your relationships and communication.

Mindfulness and positivity are intertwined. When you practice mindfulness, you become more aware of your thought patterns, especially any negative or self-critical tendencies. This awareness enables you to challenge and alter those negative thoughts, promoting a more positive mindset. Cultivating mindfulness is a journey that unfolds over time. It's not about achieving a perfect state of mindfulness but rather about continually returning to the present moment with an open heart and mind. As you integrate mindfulness into your life, you'll find it becomes a powerful tool for nurturing positivity and creating a deep sense of well-being.

Understanding the essence of mindfulness and its principles provides a solid foundation for embracing this useful practice. Mindfulness allows you to create a positive mindset by maintaining present-moment awareness, reducing stress, and enhancing emotional regulation. It empowers you to become an active participant in your thoughts and emotions, ultimately leading to a more positive and fulfilling life.

We will now focus on applicable techniques and practices that you can begin to use in your life. Incorporating mindfulness into your daily life can significantly contribute to nurturing a positive mindset. Here, we explore various mindfulness practices that you can easily integrate into your routine. These techniques empower you to embrace positivity, reduce stress, and enhance your overall well-being.

Here are ten techniques that you can begin to employ:

1. Mindful Breathing

One of the simplest yet most effective mindfulness practices is mindful breathing. Find a quiet place, sit comfortably, and focus your attention on your breath. Inhale deeply through your nose, feeling the air fill your lungs, and exhale slowly through your mouth. Pay attention to the sensation of each breath, the rise and fall of your chest, and the rhythmic flow of air. If your mind wanders, gently bring your focus back to your breath. This practice can be done for a few minutes anytime during your day to center yourself and reduce stress.

2. Body Scan Meditation

Body scan meditation is a technique that involves systematically scanning your body from head to toe with focused attention. Start by bringing your awareness to the top of your head and slowly move it down, noticing any sensations, tension, or discomfort. This practice helps you become more attuned to physical sensations and promotes relaxation. It's particularly helpful in releasing tension and promoting positive feelings.

3. Mindful Walking

Transform your daily walk into a mindfulness practice. As you walk, pay attention to the sensation of each step, the feeling of your feet connecting with the ground, and the movement of your body. Engage your senses—notice the sights, sounds, and smells around you. By staying present during your walk, you can turn it into a calming and rejuvenating experience.

4. Gratitude Journaling

Each day, take a few moments to write down things you are grateful for in a gratitude journal. This practice shifts your focus to positive aspects of your life and encourages you to savor and appreciate them. Gratitude journaling leads to a positive outlook and reminds you of the abundance in your life.

5. Mindful Eating

Mindful eating involves savoring each bite of your meals with full awareness. Pay attention to the flavors, textures, and aromas of your food. Chew slowly and appreciate the nourishment it provides. Avoid distractions like screens or rushing through meals. Mindful eating not only enhances your enjoyment of food but also promotes mindful living.

6. Three-Minute Breathing Space

The three-minute breathing space is a brief mindfulness practice you can do anytime, anywhere. It consists of three steps:

Step 1 (Awareness): Take a minute to become aware of your thoughts, emotions, and bodily sensations. Acknowledge whatever is present without judgment.

Step 2 (Gathering): In the next minute, focus your attention on your breath. Take a few deep breaths, centering yourself in the present moment.

Step 3 (Expanding): In the final minute, expand your awareness to your entire body and surroundings. Notice the bigger picture and a sense of spaciousness.

7. Mindful Use of Technology

In our digital age, it's essential to practice mindful technology use. Set aside specific times to check emails, social media, or screens. During these periods, be fully present with your digital tasks. When not using technology, unplug and engage in offline activities mindfully.

8. Loving-Kindness Meditation

Loving-kindness meditation, also known as "metta" meditation, is a practice of sending love and well-wishes to yourself and others. Begin by directing loving-kindness to yourself, then to loved ones, acquaintances, and even those you may have conflicts with. This practice cultivates compassion, empathy, and positivity toward yourself and others.

9. Mindful Conversations

Practice mindful listening during conversations. Instead of planning your response or judgment, truly listen to the speaker. Pay attention to their words, tone, and emotions. Respond with empathy and kindness, causing positive and meaningful interactions.

10. Daily Reflection

End your day with a brief period of reflection. Consider the positive moments, accomplishments, and acts of kindness you experienced during the day. Reflect on how these moments made you feel and express gratitude for them. This practice encourages positive self-reflection and reinforces positivity.

Incorporating these mindfulness techniques into your daily life empowers you to maintain a positive mindset and enhance your overall well-being. You can choose the practices that resonate with you and integrate them into your routine gradually. Over time, mindfulness becomes a natural and enriching part of your daily life, generating lasting positivity and inner peace.

3.2 The Gratitude Habit

Gratitude is the cornerstone upon which a positive mindset is built. It serves as a potent catalyst for cultivating positivity in our lives. Below we will begin to look into the significance of gratitude as the foundational pillar of a positive outlook, offering an in-depth analysis of its transformative power. Gratitude is also the art of shifting our perspective from what we lack to what we have. In our fast-paced and often materialistic world, it's easy to focus on what's missing or unattained. Gratitude invites us to pause and recognize the abundance already present in our lives. This shift in perspective changes our narrative, allowing us to see the beauty, blessings, and opportunities that surround us daily.

This habit acts as a natural magnet for positivity. When we acknowledge and appreciate the positive aspects of our lives, we invite more of the same. It's as if gratitude sends a signal to the universe that says, "I value and cherish these blessings." In response, the universe often showers us with more reasons to be grateful. This positive feedback loop fuels a continuous cycle of optimism and positivity.

Practicing gratitude can strengthen our emotional resilience. When we face challenges or adversity, a grateful mindset reminds us of the resources, support systems, and inner strengths we possess. It bolsters our ability to cope with difficulties by focusing on the silver linings and the potential for growth within adversity. Gratitude becomes a shield against despair and a source of hope.

Gratitude requires mindfulness—being fully present in the moment and appreciating its gifts as we discussed in the previous section. As we become more mindful of the positive aspects of our lives, our overall awareness and presence expand. This mindfulness, in turn, extends beyond gratitude, infusing all aspects of our existence with a heightened sense of consciousness.

It is a powerful social glue. When we express gratitude to others, we strengthen our relationships and connections. It creates trust, appreciation, and a sense of belonging. The act of acknowledging someone's kindness or support deepens our bonds and creates a positive ripple effect in our social circles.

Neuroscience research reveals that practicing gratitude can physically reshape our brain's neural pathways. Regularly focusing on gratitude can strengthen the neural circuits associated with positive emotions. This rewiring of the brain enhances our ability to experience joy, contentment, and happiness. Humans have a natural tendency toward negativity bias, where we pay more attention to negative events or experiences. Gratitude serves as a powerful counterbalance to this bias.

It encourages us to intentionally notice and celebrate positive moments, counteracting the weight of negativity. Gratitude extends inward as well. When we appreciate ourselves and recognize our accomplishments, no matter how small, we nurture self-compassion. This self-compassion is a vital component of a positive mindset, allowing us to treat ourselves with kindness and understanding.

Studies consistently show that individuals who practice this habit experience elevated levels of well-being. They report greater life satisfaction, increased happiness, and improved overall mental health. Gratitude acts as a natural antidepressant, leading to a sense of fulfillment and contentment.

Incorporating gratitude into our daily lives transforms it into a ritual of positivity. By setting aside a few moments each day to reflect on what we are grateful for, we infuse our routines with a sense of joy and appreciation. This daily habit establishes a foundation of positivity that permeates every aspect of our existence.

Fundamentally, gratitude is the compass that guides us toward a positive mindset. It empowers us to navigate life's challenges with grace, celebrate its beauty with joy, and cherish the richness of our experiences. By embracing gratitude as a foundational practice, we not only cultivate positivity but also embark on a lifelong journey of gratitude's power. It is through gratitude that we discover the true abundance that surrounds us and uncover the infinite possibilities for positivity in our lives.

Cultivating gratitude is a daily practice that can profoundly transform your mindset and outlook on life. Here are some simple yet powerful gratitude exercises and rituals to help you embrace gratitude as a regular part of your life:

Gratitude Journaling: Set aside a few minutes each day to write down three things you are grateful for. These can be simple pleasures, moments of kindness, or positive experiences. Reflect on why you appreciate them.

Morning Gratitude: Start your day by expressing gratitude. As you wake up, think of one thing you are grateful for. It could be the warmth of the sun, a cozy bed, or the prospect of a new day.

Three Good Things: Before going to bed, recall three good things that happened during the day. Reflect on why they made you feel grateful and appreciative.

The Gratitude Walk: Take a mindful walk in nature or around your neighborhood. As you walk, focus on the beauty around you—the colors of flowers, the sound of birds, or the feeling of fresh air. Express gratitude for the natural world.

Gratitude Affirmations: Create gratitude affirmations that resonate with you. For example, "I am grateful for the abundance in my life" or "I appreciate the love and support of my family." Repeat these affirmations throughout the day.

Mealtime Gratitude: Before each meal, take a moment to express gratitude for the food you are about to enjoy. Consider the journey of the food from its source to your plate and appreciate it fully.

The Gratitude Jar: Keep a gratitude jar or box. Whenever something makes you feel grateful, write it down on a slip of paper and put it in the jar. Over time, you'll have a collection of positive moments to revisit.

Gratitude Meditation: Dedicate a few minutes to a gratitude meditation. Focus on your breath and bring to mind the people, experiences, and blessings you are grateful for. Feel the warmth of gratitude filling your heart.

Thank-You Notes: Write thank-you notes or messages of appreciation to friends, family members, or colleagues. Let them know how much you value their presence or kindness in your life.

Gratitude Visualizations: Close your eyes and visualize a future filled with even more blessings and positive experiences. Imagine the joy and gratitude you will feel when these manifestations come to fruition.

Remember that consistency is key to reaping the full benefits of gratitude. Choose the exercises that resonate with you the most and incorporate them into your daily routine. Eventually over time, you'll find that gratitude becomes a natural and enriching part of your life, nurturing a positive mindset and a deeper appreciation for the world around you.

3.3 Visualization for Success

Visualization is a remarkable technique that harnesses the power of your imagination to manifest your goals and aspirations. Let us begin by discussing the profound influence of visualization in helping you achieve your dreams. Here's an in-depth analysis of how visualization can be your key to success.

The act of visualizing is not merely wishful thinking; it's rooted in science. When you vividly imagine a desired outcome, your brain doesn't distinguish it from reality. This mental rehearsal activates the same neural pathways as if you were actually experiencing the scenario. The brain's plasticity allows it to adapt to this new reality, making it more likely to manifest in your life. Visualization provides clarity and focus.

When you visualize your goals, you define them with precision. This clarity empowers you to set specific, achievable targets. It navigates you toward your objectives with unwavering determination. Visualization is a powerful tool for overcoming obstacles. By envisioning challenges and visualizing how you'll navigate them successfully, you prepare your mind to handle setbacks with resilience.

This mental rehearsal equips you with problem-solving strategies, making you more adaptable in the face of adversity. It also fuels motivation. When you vividly see yourself achieving your goals, you stoke the fires of motivation within. The mental image of success serves as a constant reminder of your aspirations, driving you to take consistent action.

Reducing anxiety is also critical to improving our lives and visualization practices can drastically do this as well. As you visualize success, you create a positive association with your goals. This counters the anxiety that often accompanies ambitious endeavors. Your mind begins to view challenges as opportunities rather than threats. As well as reducing anxiety it also bolsters self-belief. By repeatedly seeing yourself succeed, you reinforce your confidence in your abilities. This newfound self-belief becomes a powerful force in achieving your goals.

Effective visualization involves a structured process:

Clarity: Clearly define your goal. What do you want to achieve, and why is it important to you? Will it improve your life?

Imagination: Create a vivid mental image of your success. Visualize the details, emotions, and sensory experiences associated with achieving your goal.

Emotion: Infuse your visualization with strong positive emotions. Feel the joy, satisfaction, and pride of achieving your goal.

Consistency: Practice visualization regularly. Dedicate time each day to immerse yourself in your mental movie of success.

Visualize not only the end result but also the journey. Picture yourself taking consistent, purposeful steps toward your goal. This creates a road map for your actions, helping you stay on course. Combine this technique with positive affirmations. Affirmations will reinforce your belief in your ability to achieve your goals.

Use them to enhance your visualization practice. We will discuss these in greater length in chapter five.

The process of visualization is most potent when it's followed by action. Your mental imagery should inspire concrete steps. Visualization clarifies your goals and motivates you to act, turning your dreams into reality. Countless individuals have harnessed the power of visualization to achieve extraordinary feats. From athletes breaking records to entrepreneurs building empires, the success stories of those who visualized their goals serve as compelling evidence of its effectiveness.

This new skill becomes a powerful and life-changing tool for achieving your goals. Grounded in science, it provides clarity, motivation, and resilience. By consistently practicing visualization, you activate your brain's capacity to turn your dreams into reality. Visualization isn't a passive daydream; it's an active strategy that empowers you to take purposeful steps toward your aspirations. It's a key to unlocking your potential and realizing your most cherished dreams.

Guided visualization exercises are a powerful way to tap into the potential of visualization. These exercises will help you vividly imagine and manifest your dreams. Find a quiet, comfortable space and allow yourself to fully immerse in the experience. Like before, here are some examples of its power in action.

Select exercises that resonate most with your personal goals and aspirations. Tailor your choices to match the specific objectives you wish to achieve. By doing so, you'll begin to experience firsthand the remarkable effectiveness of this process.

The Dream Home Visualization: Close your eyes and imagine your dream home in vivid detail. Picture the architecture, the surroundings, and every room's interior.

Feel the emotions of living in this space—the comfort, joy, and fulfillment. Take a mental tour, exploring every corner and space. This exercise can help clarify your aspirations and motivate you to work toward them.

Career Success Visualization: Envision yourself at the peak of your career success. Imagine the position you've achieved, the responsibilities you hold, and the impact you make. Visualize your daily tasks and interactions with colleagues. Feel the sense of accomplishment, recognition, and fulfillment. This exercise can inspire you to set and achieve ambitious career goals.

Health and Wellness Visualization: Create a mental image of yourself in perfect health and wellness. See yourself engaging in physical activities you love, maintaining a balanced diet, and radiating vitality. Feel the energy and vibrancy in your body. This visualization can motivate you to prioritize your health and make positive lifestyle choices.

The Goal Achievement Visualization: Choose a specific goal you want to achieve and visualize its successful accomplishment. See yourself taking the necessary steps, overcoming obstacles, and celebrating your achievement. Feel the satisfaction and pride of reaching your goal. This visualization can provide clarity and motivation for pursuing your ambitions.

Inner Peace and Relaxation Visualization: Immerse yourself in a visualization of inner peace and relaxation. Picture a serene natural setting, like a tranquil beach or a forest. Feel the soothing sensations of calmness and tranquility. This exercise can help you manage stress and find moments of inner peace in your daily life.

The Ideal Day Visualization: Visualize your ideal day from start to finish. Imagine your morning routine, work or activities, interactions with loved ones, and leisure time. Feel the joy and contentment of living this ideal day. This exercise can inspire you to structure your days in alignment with your aspirations.

Gratitude and Abundance Visualization: Create a mental image of an abundant life filled with blessings. Visualize all the things you are grateful for—people, experiences, achievements, and opportunities. Feel the immense gratitude and joy in your heart. This visualization can deepen your sense of appreciation and positivity.

The Financial Abundance Visualization: Visualize yourself in a state of financial abundance and security. See your bank accounts thriving, investments growing, and financial worries dissipating. Feel the freedom and peace of mind that financial abundance brings. This exercise can help you set clear financial goals and take steps to achieve them.

The Relationship Harmony Visualization: Imagine your relationships filled with love, understanding, and harmony. Picture yourself communicating openly and lovingly with your partner, family, and friends. Feel the warmth and connection in your interactions. This can inspire you to nurture and strengthen your relationships.

The Personal Growth Visualization: Envision your personal growth journey. See yourself acquiring new skills, gaining knowledge, and expanding your horizons. Visualize the challenges you overcome and the confidence you build. Feel the sense of fulfillment and self-improvement.

Consistency and belief in the power of visualization are key to its effectiveness. Dedicate time to practice these guided exercises regularly, and watch as your mental images manifest into your reality. Visualization is a potent tool for turning dreams into achievements and aspirations into reality.

Chapter 4: Overcoming Negative Thought Patterns

4.1 Identifying Negative Thought Patterns

Negative thought patterns can act as formidable barriers on our journey to mastering the art of positive thinking. The initial step towards sustained success lies in recognizing and understanding these patterns. Below, we explore some of the most prevalent patterns that often permeate our modern world.

Negative Self-Talk: Negative self-talk involves harsh and critical inner dialogue. It's the habit of constantly berating yourself, believing you're not good enough, or doubting your abilities. Common forms include self-blame, self-criticism, and self-doubt.

Catastrophizing: Catastrophizing is the tendency to imagine the worst possible outcomes in any situation. You might exaggerate the potential consequences of a mistake or expect the worst in uncertain circumstances. This pattern can lead to anxiety and unnecessary stress.

All-or-Nothing Thinking: All-or-nothing thinking, also known as black-and-white thinking, involves seeing situations in extreme terms with no middle ground. You perceive things as either perfect or a complete failure, leaving no room for nuance or gradual progress.

Mind Reading: Mind reading is when you assume you know what others are thinking about you or a situation, usually in a negative way. You might believe that people are judging you or disapproving of your actions without any evidence.

Overgeneralization: Overgeneralization is when you draw sweeping conclusions based on a single negative event or experience. For example, if you fail at one task, you might generalize it to mean you're a failure in all aspects of life.

Discounting the Positive: This pattern involves dismissing or minimizing positive experiences, compliments, or achievements. You might explain them away as luck, downplay their significance, or believe you don't deserve them.

Emotional Reasoning: Emotional reasoning occurs when you believe your emotions reflect objective reality. For instance, if you feel anxious, you might conclude that there must be something genuinely threatening in your environment, even if no evidence supports it.

Should Statements: Should statements involve imposing rigid and unrealistic expectations on yourself or others. You may use words like "should," "must," or "ought to" and become frustrated or disappointed when these expectations aren't met.

Labeling and Labeling Others: Labeling is when you attach negative labels or judgments to yourself or others based on behavior or mistakes. For example, you might label yourself as a "failure" for making a mistake. Labeling others can lead to unfair judgments and prejudice.

Personalization: Personalization occurs when you take responsibility for events or outcomes that are beyond your control. You might blame yourself for external circumstances or believe that you're the cause of others' actions.

Recognizing these common negative thought patterns is the first measure in breaking free from their grip. By becoming aware of when and how they manifest in your thinking, you gain the power to challenge and modify them. As you embark on the journey of mastering the power of positive thinking, it's essential to recognize that negative thought patterns can be formidable obstacles along the way. The first thing to do for lasting success is becoming aware of these patterns in your own thinking.

In the realm of restructuring negative thought patterns to cultivate a more positive outlook, a multitude of techniques are available. However, within the pages of this book, we narrow our focus to the five most potent practices I've uncovered in my research. This deliberate choice allows you to embark on a journey of conquering self-limiting beliefs with clarity and ease.

Awareness and Mindfulness: These are foundational practices for identifying negative thought patterns. Mindfulness involves paying non-judgmental attention to your thoughts, emotions, and sensations as they arise in the present moment. By cultivating mindfulness, you can become acutely aware of your thought patterns as they unfold.

This practice encourages you to observe your thoughts without immediately reacting to them. It allows you to notice recurring negative patterns and thought loops, providing valuable insights into your mental processes. Mindfulness meditation exercises, focusing on your breath, body sensations, or the sounds around you, can strengthen your awareness muscle over time. This heightened self-awareness is the first step towards recognizing and managing negative thought patterns effectively.

Journaling: Keeping a journal is a potent tool for uncovering and understanding negative thought patterns. When you regularly record your thoughts, emotions, and experiences, you create a tangible record of your mental landscape. Journaling prompts you to reflect on your day, pinpoint moments of stress, anxiety, or self-doubt, and trace them back to the underlying thoughts that triggered these emotions.

It enables you to identify repetitive thought patterns, themes, and triggers. Additionally, journaling provides a safe space to challenge these negative thoughts, offering a proactive way to replace them with more positive and constructive alternatives. Over time, this practice helps you gain clarity about your thought processes and their impact on your overall well-being.

Cognitive Distortion Worksheets: Cognitive distortion worksheets are structured tools designed to uncover and challenge common negative thought patterns, known as cognitive distortions. These worksheets often include a list of cognitive distortions such as black-and-white thinking, catastrophizing, or personalization. By working through these worksheets, you systematically examine your thoughts and assess whether they align with any of these distortions.

This process encourages critical thinking and self-reflection, allowing you to recognize when your thoughts exhibit these distortions. It also prompts you to change these thoughts by considering more balanced and realistic perspectives. Cognitive distortion worksheets offer a structured and evidence-based approach to identifying and addressing negative thought patterns.

Feedback from Others: Seeking feedback from trusted friends, family members, or a therapist can provide invaluable insights into your thought patterns from an external perspective. Often, those close to you can observe recurring patterns in your thinking that you may not be fully aware of. They can offer objective feedback on how you tend to react to various situations, stressors, or challenges.

By engaging in open and honest conversations with others, you can gain fresh perspectives on your thought processes and their impact on your behavior and emotions. External feedback serves as a mirror that reflects your patterns and can motivate you to explore and address negative thought patterns more effectively.

Group Discussions: Engaging in group talk or support networks focused on recognizing and managing negative thought patterns can be a powerful learning experience. These groups provide a platform for individuals to share their personal experiences and insights. By listening to other individuals' stories and challenges, you can gain a broader understanding of common negative thought patterns that people often face.

Group discussions encourage self-reflection as you relate their experiences to your own. It's an opportunity to receive encouragement, support, and practical tips from peers who may have successfully tackled similar thought patterns. The collective wisdom of a group can inspire you to take proactive steps toward identifying and changing your negative thought patterns, fostering a sense of community and growth.

These five methods have consistently demonstrated their effectiveness in facilitating lasting change. However, there's no need to feel overwhelmed or compelled to adopt them all at once. Instead, consider selecting one or two methods that resonate with you based on your unique preferences and requirements. Think of it as a sliding scale, where the more time and effort you invest, the swifter and more profound the changes will manifest in your life.

As we bring this subchapter to a close, we'll explore just a few examples of self-sabotaging beliefs that individuals frequently carry with them, much like we've discovered how negative thought patterns can influence our lives. We can see why these beliefs serve no purpose other than to constrain our thinking and discuss strategies for removing them from our lives.

A common belief people may have is "I'm not good enough". This belief involves constantly doubting your abilities and feeling unworthy of success or happiness. It can lead to a lack of self-confidence and prevent you from pursuing opportunities because you assume you'll inevitably fail. Overcoming this belief requires building self-esteem and recognizing your inherent worthiness.

Another example may be "I'll always be a victim". This belief keeps individuals trapped in a victim mentality, making it difficult to break free from negative circumstances. It can hinder personal growth and resilience. Overcoming it involves acknowledging past challenges while focusing on empowerment and taking proactive steps toward a more positive future.

Then there are those who try to live in perfection thinking "I must be perfect". Where you must be flawless in every aspect of your life. It leads to unrealistic expectations and fear of making mistakes. People with this belief often procrastinate or avoid taking risks to avoid potential imperfections. Overcoming it involves embracing imperfection and understanding that growth comes from learning through mistakes.

We have highlighted just three common examples of self-sabotaging beliefs, acknowledging their presence in our lives without dwelling on negativity. It's important to recognize that the spectrum of these limiting beliefs is vast and as diverse as the individuals who hold them.

Each person may have their own unique set of beliefs that occasionally infiltrate their thoughts. However, the same techniques we've explored for mitigating negative thought patterns can also be applied to conquer these self-sabotaging beliefs. By doing so, we empower ourselves to embrace a more positive and fulfilling mindset. Awareness is key.

4.2 Strategies for Breaking Free

Cognitive behavioral techniques can be a highly effective approach for identifying and altering our negative thoughts and beliefs. It operates on the principle that our thoughts, feelings, and behaviors are interconnected. In the context of reframing negative thoughts, CBT offers many valuable techniques to challenge and transform unhelpful thought patterns.

If you have chosen to keep a thought journal to record these negative thoughts as soon as they present themselves this is often referred to as thought monitoring. Note the triggering events, the thoughts themselves, associated emotions, and any resulting behaviors. This practice allows you to identify patterns and triggers. Once identified, begin to cognitively restructure these thoughts.

This method involves examining these thoughts for cognitive distortions—irrational or exaggerated thinking patterns. Common distortions include all-or-nothing thinking, catastrophizing, and personalization that we discussed at the start of this chapter. By recognizing distortions, you can challenge the validity of these thoughts and replace them with more balanced and realistic alternatives.

One of my personal favorite techniques is asking yourself a series of probing questions to explore the validity and evidence supporting negative thoughts. Questions like, "Is this thought based on facts or am I assuming this?" and "What's the worst that can happen, and is it even likely to happen?" encourage critical thinking and help you gain a more objective perspective. This is often referred to as Socratic questioning.

Behavioral experiments can also prove to be vastly effective at restructuring our patterns of thinking. These involve testing the validity of your negative thoughts through real-world actions. For example, if you have a negative belief about social interactions, you might conduct an experiment by attending a social event and observing the actual outcomes. This provides concrete evidence to challenge negative thought patterns. This practice can work hand in hand with graded exposure techniques.

Graded exposure is particularly useful for overcoming anxiety-related negative thoughts. It involves gradually exposing yourself to feared or anxiety-inducing situations in a controlled manner. Over time, this helps desensitize you to the fear and challenges the accuracy of negative predictions.

Another practice I hold in high regard and strongly recommend is daily meditation. Meditation teaches you to create distance from your thoughts, reducing their emotional impact. The realm of meditation is vast, encompassing numerous specialized categories beyond the scope of this book. If you haven't explored a particular form of meditation, I wholeheartedly encourage you to research this field, which is now unequivocally supported by scientific research.

These cognitive-behavioral techniques provide a structured and evidence-based approach to reframing negative thoughts. By implementing these strategies, you can gain greater control over your thought processes, challenge self-limiting beliefs, and keep a more positive and resilient mindset.

In this chapter we have explored a multitude of strategies for recognizing and reframing negative thought patterns. This journey of self-awareness and transformation is a crucial foundation for what lies ahead in our understanding of the topics presented in the following pages. In the next chapter, we will gain a further understanding of how to apply the powerful tools of affirmations and positive self-talk. These practices harness the innate potential of our thoughts to shape our reality and influence our lives profoundly.

Just as we have learned to identify and reframe negative thoughts, we will now harness the positive potential of our minds. Join us as we embark on a discussion of self-empowerment and embrace the profound impact that affirmations and positive self-talk can have on our mindset and well-being.

Chapter 5: The Power of Affirmations

5.1 Harnessing the Power of Affirmations

Affirmations are concise, positive statements that are designed to influence your thoughts, emotions, and behaviors. They are declarations of intent that affirm a desired belief, outcome, or state of being. Affirmations can be used to reprogram your subconscious mind, instill positive beliefs, and reinforce constructive thought patterns.

The effectiveness of affirmations lies in their ability to reshape your cognitive landscape and rewire your mindset. Your subconscious mind is responsible for much of your automatic thoughts, beliefs, and behaviors. It operates on the information it has absorbed over time. Affirmations introduce new, positive information into the subconscious. When repeated consistently, they replace old, negative thought patterns with more constructive ones.

They also shift your focus from dwelling on problems and limitations to envisioning solutions and possibilities. They encourage a positive frame of mind, creating optimism and resilience. Repetition is key to the effectiveness of affirmations.

Each time you recite an affirmation, you reinforce the neural pathways associated with that statement. Over time, these pathways become stronger, making the positive belief more ingrained in your thinking. They are most powerful when they evoke genuine emotions.

When you truly feel the emotions associated with your affirmations, they become more deeply rooted in your subconscious. Not only do they impact your thoughts and emotions but also influence your actions. They can motivate you to take positive steps toward your goals by aligning your thoughts with your desired outcomes.

Affirmations operate on the principle of the self-fulfilling prophecy. When you consistently affirm a positive belief, you begin to act in ways that align with that belief. This, in turn, increases the likelihood of the belief becoming a reality. Further, they enhance self-esteem and self-confidence by reinforcing a positive self-image and help counteract self-doubt and negative self-talk.

Affirming positive thoughts can serve as a powerful tool for resilience. During challenging times, they provide a mental anchor, reminding you of your strengths and capabilities. It's important to note that while affirmations can be potent, they are no magic solution. They work best when integrated into a holistic approach to personal growth and well-being. Let's explore the process of crafting effective affirmations and incorporating them into your daily life to harness their transformative potential fully.

Crafting Effective Affirmations

Crafting effective affirmations begins with framing them positively and in the present tense. Instead of focusing on what you want to avoid, concentrate on what you wish to achieve. This positive framing instills a sense of empowerment. Phrase your affirmations as if your desired outcomes are already true in the present moment. This technique not only enhances the effectiveness of affirmations but also aligns your mindset with your aspirations. For example, instead of saying, "I will overcome challenges," say, "I am confidently overcoming challenges every day."

To make them even more potent, it's essential to be specific about your goals and aspirations. Specificity adds clarity and concreteness to your affirmations, making them more actionable. Customize your affirmations to reflect your unique values, desires, and beliefs. The more personally meaningful an affirmation is, the more emotionally resonant it becomes.

When crafting these, ask yourself how achieving the stated belief aligns with your life and purpose. For instance, instead of a generic affirmation like, "I am happy," you might say, "I am radiating happiness and fulfillment in my daily life". While it's beneficial to stretch your beliefs lightly with affirmations, it's also important to choose affirmations that feel somewhat attainable to you.

Effective affirmations strike a balance between aspirational and believable. Engage your emotions when crafting affirmations. Imagine the desired outcomes and infuse the affirmation with the associated emotion. The more vividly you can feel the emotions tied to your affirmations, the more deeply they become rooted in your subconscious mind. Emotionally charged affirmations have a greater impact on your belief system and behavior. For example, "I am overflowing with joy, gratitude, and self-assuredness."

Affirmations often incorporate action-oriented language. Using action verbs emphasizes the proactive steps you are taking to manifest your desires. Action-oriented affirmations inspire motivation and drive. Additionally, repetition is key to your never-ending success. Consistency is crucial in creating lasting change. Repeatedly reciting your affirmations, ideally on a daily basis, reinforces the new belief and helps establish neural pathways in the brain. These pathways make the positive belief more ingrained in your thinking, making it more likely to influence your behavior and decisions.

Pairing affirmations with vivid mental imagery of success enhances their impact. Visualization not only reinforces the affirmation but also taps into the power of mental rehearsal. Imagine yourself living the affirmation and experiencing the desired outcomes. Lastly, it's essential to remain patient and persistent in your practice.

Change takes time, and so does the impact of these thought statements. Stay committed to the process, and be open to adapting and evolving your affirmations as your goals and aspirations change. Trust in the powerful potential of affirmations to reshape your mindset for positive change, and believe in their ability to guide you toward your desired future.

5.2 Reprogramming Your Subconscious Mind

The subconscious mind is the reservoir of your beliefs, habits, and automatic responses. It plays a significant role in shaping your thoughts, emotions, and actions. Affirmations can be a powerful tool to reprogram and reshape your subconscious mind.

The thoughts that you create operate based on the principle of neuroplasticity. Neuroplasticity is the brain's ability to reorganize and adapt by forming new neural connections throughout life. When you constantly repeat affirmations, you are essentially rewiring the neural pathways in your brain. These pathways carry information related to your thoughts, beliefs, and behaviors. Repetition is the key to rewiring your subconscious mind. When you repeatedly recite affirmations, you send a consistent message to your brain.

Over time, the brain begins to prioritize and strengthen the neural pathways associated with the affirmations. This process weakens the old, limiting thought patterns and reinforces the new, positive beliefs contained in the affirmations. The continual repeating of these affirmative statements will lead to a shift at the subconscious level that will further influence your thoughts, feelings, and behaviors in alignment with the new belief.

Rewiring the subconscious mind is not an overnight process. It requires consistent practice and patience. The duration it takes to notice significant changes can vary from person to person. Some changes may be subtle at first, while others may be more noticeable. These thoughts work by leveraging the brain's capacity for neuroplasticity to reprogram your subconscious mind.

Through repetition, emotional engagement, and visualization, affirmations help shift beliefs, thoughts, and behaviors toward more positive and empowering patterns. Consistency, patience, and the formation of new habits contribute to the lasting impact of affirmations on your subconscious mind. As your subconscious mind embraces the new positive beliefs, it creates a positive feedback loop. Your thoughts, emotions, and actions become more aligned with your affirmations, reinforcing the desired outcomes.

This loop further solidifies the rewiring process. While affirmations can be highly effective in rewiring your subconscious mind, it's essential to be aware that old, negative thoughts may still resurface at times. When they do, acknowledge them without judgment and gently redirect your focus. Sometimes these negative thoughts can evolve into self-limiting beliefs.

Self-limiting beliefs are those deeply ingrained thoughts that convince us we are incapable, unworthy, or bound to fail. They can hold us back from pursuing our dreams and living our best lives. Affirmations can be a powerful tool to challenge and overcome these limiting beliefs. The first step in overcoming self-limiting beliefs is to identify them the same way we overcame negative thinking patterns and self-sabotaging beliefs.

These beliefs often operate in the background, influencing our thoughts, emotions, and behaviors. Pay attention to recurring negative thoughts and feelings of self-doubt or inadequacy. These are clues to the presence of self-limiting beliefs.

Once you've identified a self-limiting belief, create an affirmation that directly contradicts it. For example, if you believe, "I'm not smart enough to succeed," the corresponding affirmation could be, "I am intelligent and capable of achieving my goals." This affirmation challenges the negative belief and replaces it with a positive, empowering statement. Repetition is key to rewiring your thought patterns.

Consistently repeat your affirmations, ideally on a daily basis. The more you recite them, the more they replace the self-limiting beliefs in your subconscious mind. Over time, your new, positive beliefs will become more deeply ingrained. Combine visualization with your affirmations. As you recite your affirmations, vividly imagine yourself living the belief contained in the affirmation.

Visualize yourself confidently taking action, achieving your goals, and breaking free from the limitations of the old belief. Remember to engage your emotions when working with affirmations to overcome self-limiting beliefs. Connect with the emotions associated with your new, empowering beliefs.

Feel the confidence, self-worth, and determination that these affirmations bring. Emotional resonance strengthens the impact of the affirmations. Overcoming self-limiting beliefs is a process that may take time. Be patient with yourself and acknowledge small victories along the way.

As you consistently use affirmations, you'll notice a shift in your thinking and behavior, indicating progress in overcoming these limitations. Shape your affirmations to address specific self-limiting beliefs. If you have multiple, create affirmations for each one. The more targeted the affirmation, the more effective it is at dismantling the associated belief.

Sometimes, working with a therapist or coach can provide valuable support in identifying and overcoming deep-seated self-limiting beliefs. They can offer guidance and additional tools to help you on your journey. You can also share your affirmation practice with a trusted friend or family member who can hold you accountable.

Discussing your progress with someone can provide encouragement and motivation. Keep a journal to track your progress. Write down your affirmations, record how you feel, and note any positive changes in your thoughts and actions. This can serve as a powerful record of your transformation.

We have discussed the profound influence of affirmations in rewiring your subconscious mind and conquering any self-limiting beliefs. Affirmations, through their power of repetition, emotional resonance, and visualization, serve as a bridge to a new, empowered self. They reshape the very fabric of your thinking, instilling beliefs that nurture your potential and aspirations.

This transformative process is not merely about self-affirmation but a dynamic journey of self-discovery and personal growth. As you continue to embrace the potential of affirmations, the boundaries of what you once believed possible expand, leading you toward a future rich with promise and possibility.

Chapter 6: Navigating Challenges With Resilience

6.1 The Importance of Resilience

Resilience is a fundamental pillar in the framework of positive thinking, weaving seamlessly into the tapestry of personal growth and transformation. It serves as a steadfast companion on the journey of embracing a positive mindset. Resilience is the ability to bounce back from adversity, setbacks, and life's inevitable challenges with unwavering determination and adaptability.

In the context of this book, positive thinking is not about avoiding challenges or living in a perpetual state of optimism. Instead, it's about facing life's complexities with a mindset that empowers you to see opportunities in difficulties, to learn and grow from failures, and to maintain hope in the face of uncertainty.

Resilience is the backbone of this approach. It equips you with the mental fortitude to confront setbacks as stepping stones, not stumbling blocks, in your path to personal development.

Positive thinking and resilience are interdependent on each other. Thinking positively fuels resilience by creating a belief in your capacity to overcome obstacles. Conversely, resilience bolsters positive thinking by providing the strength to maintain a hopeful outlook, even when confronted with adversity. Together, they form a dynamic synergy that propels you forward in the pursuit of your goals and aspirations.

Resilience serves as an indispensable companion on the path of positive thinking, enhancing our ability to confront and triumph over life's challenges. It acts as a dynamic force that fuels our commitment to maintaining an optimistic outlook, even when faced with adversity.

At its core, positive thinking is not an avoidance of life's complexities or an unwarranted denial of difficulties. Instead, it equips us with the mental agility to view obstacles as opportunities, to extract valuable lessons from setbacks, and to maintain unwavering hope in the face of uncertainty.

So far we have embraced positive thinking as a mindset that empowers us to navigate life's intricacies with grace and resilience. Resilience, in turn, bolsters our positive thinking by providing the emotional and mental strength required to face challenges head-on.

It instills in us the belief that we possess the inner resources and determination to overcome hurdles and emerge stronger on the other side. Together, resilience and positive thinking form a harmonious partnership that propels us forward in our pursuit of personal development and a fulfilling life.

As we continue, we will explore the profound role resilience plays in not only weathering storms but also thriving amid them. We will uncover practical strategies and insights to help us navigate life's challenges with determination, adaptability, and a steadfast faith in our capacity to not only endure but also flourish.

Remember, resilience is not merely a tool for survival; it is a potent catalyst for growth and success, aligning seamlessly with the principles of positive thinking that have guided us on this journey.

6.2 Strategies for Building Resilience

Cultivating a growth mindset is a great practice that significantly contributes to resilience. At its core, a growth mindset is the belief that abilities and intelligence can be developed through dedication, effort, and learning. In contrast, a fixed mindset assumes that abilities are innate and unchangeable. Understanding and adopting a growth mindset is pivotal in the pursuit of a resilient mindset for several reasons.

Individuals with a growth mindset tend to view challenges as opportunities for growth and learning. Instead of shying away from difficulties, they see them as a chance to develop new skills, gain experience, and expand their capabilities. This perspective allows them to approach challenges with enthusiasm rather than fear, making them more resilient in the face of adversity.

A growth mindset leads us to adaptability and flexibility. Those who believe in the potential for growth are more willing to adapt to changing circumstances and explore different strategies when faced with setbacks. This adaptability is a crucial component of resilience, as it enables individuals to navigate obstacles with a sense of resourcefulness and a willingness to try new approaches.

It is not merely about bouncing back from adversity but also about learning from it. Individuals with a growth mindset approach setbacks as valuable learning experiences. They extract lessons from their challenges, which empowers them to better navigate similar situations in the future. This continual learning and self-improvement are hallmarks of resilient individuals.

This state of mind encourages persistence and determination. When individuals believe that effort and dedication can lead to improvement, they are more likely to persevere in the face of difficulties. This unwavering determination is a key characteristic of resilience, as it allows individuals to keep moving forward even when the path is challenging.

Cultivating a growth mindset is not just about adopting a new belief; it's about putting that belief into action. Resilience is not a passive trait but an active one, and a growth mindset motivates individuals to take proactive steps to overcome challenges and achieve their goals. Practical steps you can take to strengthen this mindset include, but not limited to, the following:

Embrace Challenges with Enthusiasm:

- Approach challenges as opportunities for growth and self-improvement.
- Reframe setbacks as stepping stones toward your goals.
- Recognize that facing difficulties head-on can lead to personal development and greater resilience.

Cultivate a Love for Learning:

- Develop a genuine curiosity and hunger for knowledge.
- See each experience, whether successful or not, as a chance to learn.
- Continually seek out opportunities to expand your skills and expertise.

Emphasize Effort and Persistence:

- Shift your focus from innate talent to the effort you put forth.
- Understand that sustained effort and determination are the keys to improvement.
- Embrace challenges that push you beyond your comfort zone.

Embrace Mistakes and Setbacks:

- View mistakes as valuable learning experiences.
- Understand that setbacks are part of the journey toward growth
- Analyze failures to extract lessons and insights for future success.

Maintain a Positive Self-Image:

- Develop a healthy self-esteem based on your growth and accomplishments.
- Avoid self-criticism and instead practice self-compassion.
- Celebrate your progress, no matter how small it may seem.

Seek Feedback and Constructive Criticism:

- Solicit feedback from others to gain different perspectives.
- Welcome constructive criticism as a means to improve.
- Use feedback as a tool for growth and refinement.

Set Ambitious but Realistic Goals:

- Challenge yourself with ambitious goals that align with your values.
- Break these goals into smaller, achievable steps.
- Track your progress and celebrate your successes along the way.

Surround Yourself with Growth-Oriented Individuals:

- Associate with people who share a growth mindset.
- Engage in discussions and collaborations that promote learning and development.
- Draw inspiration from the achievements and journeys of others.

Practice Mindfulness and Self-Reflection:

- Cultivate mindfulness to stay present and focused on your growth journey.
- Regularly reflect on your experiences, challenges, and progress.
- Use mindfulness techniques to manage stress and maintain emotional balance.

Developing this growth mindset is an ongoing process that requires intention and practice. By incorporating these practical steps into your daily life, you'll not only strengthen your belief in your capacity to grow and thrive but also enhance your resilience in the face of life's challenges. This resilient mindset, rooted in the belief that you can adapt, learn, and flourish, will empower you to navigate obstacles with confidence and determination.

Embracing Challenge

Embracing challenges as opportunities can be another powerful tool in your arsenal that empowers you to navigate life's complexities with resilience and a growth-oriented perspective. Here, we'll explore this concept further and discuss how it relates to building resilience within the context of positive thinking. It involves a fundamental shift in perspective.

Instead of viewing difficulties as roadblocks or threats, you see them as chances to learn, grow, and evolve. This shift is at the heart of resilience, as it allows you to approach adversity with a sense of curiosity and optimism. These challenges often push individuals out of their comfort zones, encouraging personal growth. When you confront difficulties head-on, you discover hidden strengths, develop new skills, and gain valuable experiences. This continuous process of self-improvement is a cornerstone of resilience.

Resilient individuals not only endure challenges but also learn from them. They analyze setbacks, failures, and obstacles to extract lessons and insights. This learning not only equips them to overcome similar challenges in the future but also reinforces their belief in their capacity to adapt and thrive. Successfully embracing challenges bolsters confidence and self-esteem. Each time you overcome a hurdle, you gain confidence in your abilities.

This self-assurance becomes a powerful asset as you face increasingly complex challenges, generating a sense of resilience and self-belief. Resilience is also closely linked to adaptability. When you embrace challenges, you develop the ability to adapt to changing circumstances and find innovative solutions. This adaptability enables you to weather storms and pivot when necessary, contributing to your overall resilience.

Difficulties in life can be powerful motivators. They provide a sense of purpose and direction, driving you to pursue your goals with determination. Resilient individuals use these challenges as fuel to propel themselves forward, even when the path ahead seems uncertain. Embracing challenges aligns seamlessly with cultivating a growth mindset. Both concepts emphasize the belief that abilities and intelligence can be developed through effort and learning. This mindset not only enhances resilience but also nurtures a positive thinking approach to life's difficult situations.

This is not a passive endeavor; it's a proactive approach to life. Resilient individuals actively seek out opportunities to test their limits, take calculated risks, and embrace uncertainty. They view each challenge as a chance to write a new chapter in their growth story.

By following the advice of this chapter, you position yourself to increase resilience that is deeply rooted in the belief that you have the capacity to adapt, learn, and thrive, no matter what life presents. This mindset empowers you to face adversity with courage, transform setbacks into stepping stones, and maintain an unwavering belief in your ability to navigate life's twists and turns.

Chapter 7: Positive Relationships

7.1 The Impact of Positivity on Relationships

Positive relationships are not just a component of life instead they are the very essence that gives life depth, meaning, and vibrancy. These connections weave a rich tapestry that encompasses a diverse spectrum of individuals, from cherished friends and beloved family members to romantic partners who hold our hearts and colleagues who accompany us on our professional journey.

Beyond these close-knit circles, positive relationships extend their benevolent influence to embrace the broader community, creating a ripple effect of goodwill and shared positivity. The impact of positivity within these relationships is nothing short of profound, touching every facet of our existence, and its reach is far-reaching, echoing through our personal history.

Within the warm embrace of positive relationships, we find the solace of understanding, the strength of shared experiences, and the power to uplift one another. These connections form a refuge where communication thrives, trust deepens, and vulnerability finds a safe haven. In such an environment, words become bridges, not barriers. Honesty becomes the currency of trust and vulnerability becomes the touchstone of genuine connection.

Moreover, positive relationships provide us with resilience—a vital armor that shields us during turbulent times. Conflicts and challenges cease to be harbingers of discord; instead, they become opportunities for growth, understanding, and deeper connection. Through the ebbs and flows of life, these relationships stand steadfast, offering unwavering support and a shoulder to lean on.

The impact of positivity within these bonds extends beyond the emotional realm. It stretches into the physical and mental dimensions of our well-being, reducing stress levels, nurturing cardiovascular health, and lighting the path to emotional equilibrium. In the cocoon of positive relationships, we find solace, strength, and the nourishment of our soul.

As we embark on this chapter, we will explore the profound impact of positivity on relationships in greater depth. We will dive into the intricacies of creating positive connections, nurturing them, and allowing them to flourish, unlocking their transformative potential to enhance our well-being, resilience, and overall quality of life. Join us as we unveil the art of cultivating positive relationships—a journey that promises to enrich every facet of your existence.

The influence of a positive mindset on our relationships is deep and expansive. In the following words, we will explore the remarkable potency of positivity in shaping and sustaining our connections, unveiling its role in building and nurturing relationships.

Enhanced Communication: Positivity creates open and effective communication. When individuals engage in positive and constructive conversations, they are more likely to express their thoughts and emotions, listen actively, and resolve conflicts amicably. This leads to healthier, more meaningful relationships.

Trust: Positive relationships are built on trust, which forms the foundation of any deep and lasting connection. Positivity engenders trust by promoting honesty, reliability, and emotional safety. In such an environment, individuals feel comfortable being vulnerable and sharing their true selves.

Resilience in Conflict: Positivity equips individuals and relationships with resilience during challenging times. When positivity prevails, conflicts are approached as opportunities for growth and understanding, rather than as destructive forces. This approach allows couples, families, and friends to navigate adversity with grace and unity.

Supportive Networks: Positive relationships create a robust support system. Friends and loved ones who radiate positivity are more likely to provide emotional, practical, and moral support during difficult times. These supportive networks become invaluable resources for individuals seeking encouragement and assistance.

Health and Well-Being: The impact of positivity extends to physical and mental health. Positive relationships have been linked to lower stress levels, improved cardiovascular health, and enhanced emotional well-being. The emotional support derived from positive relationships is also a vital aspect of overall health.

Nurtured Growth: In positive relationships, individuals are encouraged to grow and evolve. Partners, family members, and friends who embrace positivity often inspire one another to pursue personal development, chase dreams, and explore new horizons.

Creating Happy Memories: Positivity leads to the creation of cherished memories. Positive interactions, shared laughter, and joyful moments become lasting imprints of relationships. These memories provide a wellspring of happiness to draw upon during challenging times.

Longevity: Positive relationships contribute to longevity. Numerous studies have shown that individuals with strong social connections and positive relationships tend to live longer, healthier lives. The emotional support and sense of purpose provided by positive relationships are vital components of this effect.

Cultivating Resilience: Positivity within relationships nurtures resilience as well. It bolsters individuals' ability to bounce back from setbacks, persevere through difficulties, and find strength in the love and support of their social circles.

A Fulfilling Life: Ultimately, positivity within relationships enriches life. It adds depth, meaning, and happiness to each day. Positive relationships are a source of joy, laughter, and shared experiences, making life more vibrant and fulfilling.

In our lives, the impact of positivity on relationships is nothing short of profound. As we've traversed this chapter, we've uncovered the radiant influence that a positive mindset can have on our connections, whether they be with cherished friends, beloved family members, life partners, or the expansive web of our broader community. Positivity, in its essence, serves as the cornerstone upon which the most fulfilling and enduring relationships are built.

It is the unspoken language that generates understanding, the currency of trust that strengthens bonds, and the resilient shield that defends connections during the turbulent storms of life. In essence, positivity imbues our relationships with a profound sense of warmth, resilience, and shared joy.

As we turn the page to the chapters ahead, we carry with us the wisdom of this profound impact. With each lesson, we unveil the potential that positivity holds, empowering us to cultivate relationships that not only endure but also thrive. Through practical strategies and insights, we will embark on a journey to infuse our connections with positivity, enriching our lives and those of our loved ones.

7.2 Effective Communication

Effective communication forms the bedrock of healthy and positive relationships. It is the bridge that connects individuals, allowing them to share thoughts, feelings, and experiences with clarity and compassion. In positive relationships, communication is more than just a means of conveying information; it is a dynamic process that creates trust, deepens connections, and resolves conflicts constructively. When individuals engage in open, honest, and respectful communication, they form an environment where positivity thrives. Positive communication sets the stage for affirming interactions, mutual understanding, and the nurturing of bonds that stand the test of time.

One aspect of this is active listening. It is a cornerstone of effective communication, and its role in maintaining positivity within relationships cannot be overstated. It goes beyond merely hearing words; it involves fully engaging with the speaker, paying attention to their words, tone, and body language. Active listening communicates a deep level of respect and empathy, showing that you value the speaker's perspective and feelings.

In a positive relationship, active listening creates space for individuals to express themselves without judgment, promoting trust and emotional safety. It allows partners, friends, or family members to feel heard and understood, paving the way for constructive and harmonious interactions.

Empathy and understanding are inseparable from positivity within relationships. Empathy involves stepping into another person's shoes, experiencing their emotions, and validating their feelings. It is the ability to connect on a profound level, recognizing humanity in one another. In a positive relationship, empathy creates an atmosphere of compassion and support. It acknowledges that every individual's experience is unique and deserving of acknowledgment.

Understanding, on the other hand, is the result of empathy and active listening. It is the bridge that connects two people, allowing them to relate to each other's experiences and perspectives. When individuals in a relationship cultivate empathy and understanding, they foster a sense of unity, reducing conflicts and promoting positivity.

Positivity, in this context, thrives when effective communication, active listening, empathy, and understanding come together. It is nurtured through conversations that are respectful, empathetic, and affirming. Positive communication sets the stage for shared joy, a deep sense of connection, and the resolution of conflicts with grace and kindness. As we explore these aspects further, we will uncover practical strategies for infusing everyday interactions with positivity, strengthening the bonds that enrich our lives.

Practicing active listening in social settings opens the door to a richer understanding of the world through someone else's lens, while also creating a sense of empathy that naturally guides us toward employing language with a more positive and optimistic tone. By truly tuning in to the thoughts, feelings, and experiences of others, we not only forge deeper connections but also gain fresh insights and appreciation for different viewpoints.

Positive language and framing are potent tools that can profoundly influence the quality of communication within relationships. Positive language involves choosing words and expressions that are constructive, optimistic, and affirming. It re-frames conversations from a focus on problems to a focus on solutions and opportunities. This shift in language not only encourages a more positive atmosphere but also enhances understanding and collaboration.

In positive relationships, individuals use positive language to express their feelings and needs, reducing defensiveness and promoting open dialogue. Moreover, positive framing involves viewing situations and challenges in a more positive light. It allows individuals to reframe difficulties as opportunities for growth and learning. When conflicts arise, positive framing encourages partners, family members, or friends to approach resolution with a spirit of cooperation and understanding.

There are instances where, despite our sincere efforts to employ positive language and maintain harmony, conflicts may still emerge. It is during these moments that we must proactively step in to address and resolve the conflict. Resolving the conflict becomes an essential skill in preserving the positivity within our relationships.

It requires us to navigate disagreements with patience, empathy, and respect, keeping in mind that conflicts can serve as opportunities for growth and deeper understanding. By approaching these challenges with a commitment to finding common ground, we can not only resolve the conflict but also reinforce the positivity and resilience of our connections.

This conflict resolution is a crucial aspect of maintaining positive relationships. It involves addressing disagreements and differences in a constructive and respectful manner. Individuals recognize that conflicts are not inherently destructive but rather opportunities for growth and understanding. Conflict resolution techniques include active listening, expressing feelings and needs clearly, and seeking compromise.

The goal is to find common ground and arrive at solutions that honor the needs and perspectives of all parties involved. Positive conflict resolution not only resolves immediate issues but also strengthens relationships by demonstrating respect, patience, and a commitment to mutual growth. It reinforces the idea that conflicts can lead to deeper understanding and greater unity.

Non-verbal communication is a vital but often overlooked aspect of effective communication within relationships. It includes body language, facial expressions, tone of voice, and gestures. In positive relationships, individuals are attuned to their non-verbal cues and those of their communication partners. They understand that non-verbal signals can convey emotions and intentions more powerfully than words alone.

Maintaining eye contact, using open and welcoming body language, and employing a warm tone of voice can create trust and enhance the overall quality of communication. Being aware of non-verbal cues in others allows individuals to better understand their emotions and respond with empathy. Positive non-verbal communication creates an environment of emotional safety and reinforces the positivity of interactions.

Up to this point, we've underscored the significance of active listening as a conduit for understanding and empathy, facilitating the use of constructive language and, when necessary, the resolution of occasional conflicts. Now, our journey takes us into the realm of diverse communication styles that contribute to the cultivation of more positive and harmonious relationships.

Effective communication within relationships encompasses not only the choice of words but also the style in which those words are delivered. Different communication styles play a pivotal role in shaping the dynamics of our interactions.

Here we will break down the various communication styles, including assertive, passive, and aggressive approaches. Understanding these styles and their implications is instrumental in creating constructive, positive, and harmonious relationships.

Assertive Communication: This form of communication involves expressing thoughts, feelings, and needs with clarity, confidence, and respect for oneself and others. It encourages open and honest dialogue. Assertiveness promotes mutual respect, encourages problem-solving, and enhances self-esteem. It evokes a sense of equality in relationships. It can be challenging to strike the right balance between assertiveness and aggression. Some may initially perceive assertiveness as confrontational.

Passive Communication: Passive communicators tend to avoid conflict and prioritize others' needs over their own. They may not express their thoughts or feelings, leading to unmet needs and misunderstandings. These individuals may avoid unnecessary conflicts, maintain a sense of harmony, and be viewed as easygoing. The suppression of one's thoughts and emotions can lead to resentment and unfulfilled needs.

Passive communication may hinder personal growth and the resolution of issues.

Aggressive Communication: These communicators express their thoughts and feelings forcefully, often at the expense of others' feelings and opinions. They may resort to shouting, blaming, or intimidation. Aggressive communication may yield immediate results but at a significant cost to relationships. It can be perceived as a means of gaining control. Aggressiveness often damages relationships, erodes trust, and generates a hostile atmosphere. It rarely leads to long-term solutions or positive outcomes.

While each communication style has its place, adopting an assertive and positive communication style is pivotal in building constructive interactions. Assertive communication allows individuals to express themselves clearly and respectfully, leading to understanding and problem-solving. It encourages mutual respect and openness within relationships.

When coupled with positivity, assertiveness becomes a powerful tool for nurturing positive connections, as it enables individuals to convey their thoughts and needs while affirming the value of others' perspectives. This combination creates an environment where conflicts are addressed with empathy and solutions are sought collaboratively, ultimately leading to more positive and harmonious relationships.

Throughout the length of this chapter, we have witnessed the profound influence of positivity within our relationships. We have discovered that positivity forms the very essence of lasting and fulfilling connections. It serves as a magnetic force that attracts individuals, drawing them closer in a tapestry of warmth and understanding.

Positivity within relationships is more than a fleeting sentiment; it is an enduring commitment to seeing the best in others, embracing their flaws and strengths alike. It is an unwavering belief in the potential for growth, both individually and together, that underpins the most enriching connections of our lives.

Nurturing these relationships infused with positivity and effective communication is an ongoing process—a process marked by understanding, empathy, and growth. It is a commitment to building connections that are rich in trust, respect, and shared joy. By embracing these principles, you will not only transform your relationships but also enrich your own life. As you apply these lessons, you'll find your relationships blossoming into vibrant tapestries of love, understanding, and positivity.

Below is a selection of practical exercises and techniques for you to incorporate into your daily life to increase communication skills while cultivating positive thinking in various relationships.

I-Statements: Use "I" statements to express your feelings and needs assertively. For example, say, "I feel frustrated when…" instead of "You always…"

Empathy Practice: Make a conscious effort to put yourself in the other person's shoes, acknowledging their feelings and experiences with empathy.

Conflict Resolution Skills: Develop conflict resolution skills such as problem-solving, compromise, and staying calm during disagreements to maintain harmony.

Non-Verbal Awareness: Pay attention to your body language, tone of voice, and facial expressions to ensure they convey warmth, respect, and positivity.

Random Acts of Kindness: Regularly perform small acts of kindness for your loved ones to create a positive, nurturing environment within your relationships.

Setting Boundaries: Establish healthy boundaries to maintain a sense of self while creating positive connections with others.

Active Problem-Solving: Approach relationship challenges as problems to be solved together, encouraging collaboration and mutual growth.

Express Appreciation: Frequently express your appreciation and gratitude to those you care about, reinforcing positive feelings in your relationships.

Forgiveness: Practice forgiveness, both for yourself and others, to release negativity and promote healing within your relationships.

Chapter 8: Goals, Dreams, And Manifestation

In this concise book, we've embarked on a journey of positive thinking, recognizing its pivotal role in shaping our lives. We've explored the science underpinning this mindset and its profound impact on our subconscious. By rewiring our thought processes, we've learned to cultivate our own positive mindset, incorporating practices like gratitude and visualization to fuel our aspirations.

Through the power of affirmations and related techniques, we've shattered the chains of negative thought patterns and self-limiting beliefs, forging a resilient and unyielding state of mind. This newfound wisdom has equipped us to infuse positivity into all our relationships, enriching our individual life paths.

As we venture into the following three chapters, our focus shifts to crafting and realizing our goals and dreams. This journey will be guided by the principles of abundance, kindness, and gratitude, which we'll integrate into our daily lives. These practices will not only lead us toward our desired destinations but also enable us to maintain a positively empowered existence, resiliently navigating the twists and turns the universe may present.

8.1 Setting and Clarifying Goals

Embarking on a journey toward personal and professional fulfillment often begins with a vision of the life you aspire to lead, the accomplishments you wish to achieve, and the person you aim to become. Yet, a vision, no matter how vivid, remains a mere aspiration until it is translated into concrete goals. Setting and clarifying these goals is the transformative bridge between envisioning your dreams and manifesting them into reality. It is a process that requires intention, precision, and a clear map for your journey.

In this chapter, we will explore the art of goal-setting and the power it holds in shaping the course of our lives. We'll introduce you to the SMART framework, a proven method for defining goals that are Specific, Measurable, Achievable, Relevant, and Time-Bound. Through this framework, you will not only gain the ability to set clear objectives but also to decipher the steps required to reach them.

Join us on this expedition into the heart of goal setting, where your dreams are transformed into achievable milestones, and your aspirations become your guiding stars.

The Smart Framework System

Specific: Your goals should be clear and precise, leaving no room for ambiguity. Clearly state what you want to achieve, who is involved, what resources are required, and where it will happen.

Measurable: Your goals should be quantifiable, allowing you to track progress and determine when you've successfully achieved them. Ask yourself questions like: How will I measure progress? How will I know when the goal is achieved?

Achievable: Ensure that your goals are realistic and attainable. While it's important to set ambitious objectives, they should still be within the realm of possibility. Consider your current resources, skills, and constraints.

Relevant: Goals should align with your broader objectives and be relevant to your life or aspirations. Ensure that pursuing these goals makes sense in the context of your values and long-term vision.

Time-Bound: Set a specific time frame for achieving your goals. Establishing deadlines creates a sense of urgency and helps you stay focused and accountable. Ask yourself: When do I want to achieve this goal?

The "S" in SMART stands for Specific, and it emphasizes the importance of setting clear, well-defined goals. Specific goals are precise and unambiguous, leaving no room for confusion or misinterpretation. When a goal is specific, you know exactly what needs to be achieved. Some key points to consider when setting specific goals are as followed:

Clarity: Ensure that your goal is crystal clear and easy to understand. It should answer the fundamental questions of who, what, where, when, and why.

Details: Include as many details as necessary to paint a vivid picture of your goal. Specify the desired outcome, any relevant tasks, and the scope of the goal.

Focus: Avoid vague or general objectives. Instead, concentrate on a particular aspect or result you want to accomplish.

Examples: Instead of a broad goal like "Improve my career," a specific goal could be "Secure a promotion to the position of Senior Project Manager within my current company by the end of the fiscal year."

The specificity of your goals helps you maintain a clear direction and stay motivated. It leaves little room for misunderstanding and provides a course for action, making it easier to track progress and measure success. By ensuring that your goals are specific, you set yourself up for greater clarity and achievement on your journey.

The "M" in SMART highlights the importance of making goals measurable. Measurable goals provide clear criteria for assessing progress and determining when the goal has been achieved. This step is about quantifying your objectives to track your journey effectively.

Quantify: Express your goal in terms of specific numbers, metrics, or criteria that can be objectively measured. This could include quantities, percentages, timelines, or other relevant measurements.

Track Progress: Establish methods for monitoring and tracking your progress toward the goal. Identify key milestones and indicators that will help you measure your advancement.

Define Success: Determine what success looks like. Outline the specific outcomes or results that will signify the accomplishment of your goal.

Examples: Instead of a vague goal like "Losing weight," a measurable goal could be "Lose precisely 15 pounds over the next three months by following a healthy eating plan and exercising three times a week."

Setting measurable goals empowers you to track your advancement in a concrete and objective manner. It enables you to celebrate milestones, stay motivated, and make informed adjustments to your strategies if needed. Measuring progress ensures that you remain on the right track and allows you to clearly recognize when you have successfully achieved your goal.

The "A" in SMART stands for Achievable, emphasizing the importance of setting goals that are realistic and attainable. An achievable goal is one that can be realistically accomplished, given your available resources, skills, and constraints.

Assessing Resources: Evaluate the resources and tools you have at your disposal. Consider whether you have the time, money, knowledge, and support necessary to pursue the goal.

Realistic Expectations: Ensure that your goal is within the realm of possibility. While it's essential to aim high, setting overly ambitious goals that are beyond your current capabilities can lead to frustration.

Challenges and Growth: An achievable goal may still present challenges and require effort, but it should be a challenge you believe you can overcome with dedication and persistence.

Examples: Instead of an unrealistic goal like "Become a professional athlete within a year," an achievable goal could be "Complete a half-marathon race in nine months after consistent training and preparation."

Setting achievable goals sets you up for success by ensuring that your objectives are within reach. It prevents discouragement and maintains your motivation as you work toward your goal. An achievable goal is challenging but attainable, allowing you to stretch your capabilities while remaining grounded in reality.

The "R" in SMART underscores the importance of setting goals that are relevant and aligned with your broader objectives and values. Relevant goals should make sense in the context of your life and aspirations, ensuring that your efforts are meaningful and purposeful.

Alignment: Ensure that the goal aligns with your personal values, long-term vision, and overarching objectives. It should contribute to your overall aspirations and be relevant to your life's direction.

Meaningful Impact: Consider whether achieving the goal will have a meaningful impact on your life. Will it bring you closer to the life you desire, or is it merely a distraction?

Current Situation: Evaluate your current circumstances and whether pursuing the goal is appropriate at this stage of your life. Assess whether the goal is relevant to your current needs and priorities.

Examples: Instead of a goal that doesn't align with your values, such as "Spend the weekends working overtime," a relevant goal could be "Devote weekends to personal development and quality time with family, aligning with my commitment to work-life balance."

Setting relevant goals ensures that your efforts are focused on what truly matters to you. It prevents you from pursuing objectives that might lead you astray from your long-term vision. Relevant goals are meaningful and contribute to your personal growth and fulfillment.

Lastly, the "T" in SMART emphasizes the importance of setting goals with a specific time frame or deadline. A time-bound goal has a well-defined endpoint, helping to create a sense of urgency and maintain your focus on achieving the objective within a set period.

Set Deadlines: Clearly specify when you intend to achieve the goal. This could be a specific date, month, or year. Having a deadline prevents procrastination and provides a sense of urgency.

Breakdown into Milestones: Consider breaking down the goal into smaller milestones or checkpoints with their respective deadlines. This allows you to track your progress and stay on course.

Be Accountable: Share your goal and its deadline with someone you trust or create public accountability. This can enhance your commitment to achieving the goal within the specified time frame.

Examples: Instead of a vague goal like "Write a novel one day", a time-bound goal could be "Complete the first draft of my novel within the following six months, with regular writing sessions and a deadline of next year".

Setting time-bound goals provides a sense of urgency and motivation. It prevents the goal from lingering as a distant aspiration and encourages you to take consistent action toward its achievement. The presence of a deadline helps you stay focused and accountable throughout your journey.

Now that we have broken down the SMART system, dissecting its components, we're equipped to put it into action and define our personal and professional goals. This system is adaptable to every facet of our lives, guiding us to establish realistic and achievable objectives that may have once seemed out of reach. It underscores the notion that there are no limits to what we can accomplish with dedication and persistence, making even our most audacious dreams attainable through consistent effort.

Below is a more concise breakdown of the SMART system to use as a reference point while you embark on the exciting journey of setting your own distinctive goals. This framework, as we've explored in detail, is a versatile tool that empowers you to define objectives with specificity, measure progress, ensure they are achievable, align them with your values, and establish realistic deadlines.

Whether you're aiming for personal growth, career advancement, or any other aspiration, keep the SMART principles in mind as your reliable guide, ensuring that each goal you set is thoughtful, strategic, and ultimately, attainable.

The SMART Framework

Specific: Your goals should leave no room for ambiguity. They should be precise, detailing what you want to achieve, who's involved, the necessary resources, and the location or context.

Measurable: Make your goals quantifiable so you can track progress and gauge successful achievement. Consider how you'll measure progress and when you'll know the goal is attained.

Achievable: While ambition is crucial, your goals should also be realistic and attainable, taking into account your current resources, skills, and constraints.

Relevant: Align your goals with your broader objectives and life aspirations, ensuring they make sense within the context of your values and long-term vision.

Time-Bound: Set specific deadlines for your goals. These time frames create a sense of urgency, helping you maintain focus and accountability. Determine when you want to achieve each goal.

Identifying personal and professional goals is a crucial step in the journey of self-improvement and success. This process involves introspection, self-awareness, and a clear understanding of what you aspire to achieve in different aspects of your life.

Personal Goals

Self-Reflection: Begin by reflecting on your life's priorities, values, and passions. What matters most to you? What do you envision for your personal growth and fulfillment?

Short-Term vs. Long-Term: Distinguish between short-term and long-term personal goals. Short-term goals might include improving a specific skill, while long-term goals could involve achieving a life-changing aspiration like traveling the world.

Health and Well-Being: Consider setting personal goals related to your physical and mental health, such as maintaining a fitness routine, practicing mindfulness, or achieving work-life balance.

Interpersonal Relationships: Assess your relationships with family and friends. Are there goals related to strengthening these bonds, resolving conflicts, or spending quality time with loved ones?

Professional Goals

Career Aspirations: Define your professional aspirations. What position or role do you aim to achieve in your career? Are there specific industries or fields you're passionate about?

Skill Development: Identify the skills and knowledge you need to excel in your profession. Set goals to acquire these competencies through education, training, or on-the-job experience.

Networking and Growth: Consider networking and professional growth goals, such as expanding your professional network, seeking mentorship, or pursuing leadership roles.

Work-Life Balance: Reflect on your work-life balance and set goals to improve it. This may involve setting boundaries, optimizing time management, or pursuing remote work options.

Aligning Personal and Professional Goals

Balance: Strive for a balance between personal and professional goals. Ensure that one aspect of your life complements the other rather than competing against it.

Prioritization: Prioritize your goals based on their importance and feasibility. Some goals may take precedence over others at specific stages of your life.

Flexibility: Be open to adjusting your goals as circumstances change. Life is dynamic, and your objectives may need to adapt accordingly.

Identifying personal and professional goals is a process that sets the stage for meaningful growth and accomplishment. It empowers you to create a layout for your life's journey, guiding you toward a future that aligns with your values and aspirations.

Now, let's take a closer look into the practice of manifestation, exploring various methods and approaches that enable us to synchronize our thoughts, emotions, and actions. By doing so, we can transform the goals we've set into tangible reality.

8.2 The Art of Manifestation

Manifestation, in its essence, is the art of channeling the power of intention, harnessing the magnetic forces of thoughts and emotions, and aligning our actions with our deepest desires. It is the age-old practice of transforming our visions into lived experiences. Through the pages of this chapter, we will take a look into the inner workings of this profound phenomenon, unlocking the secrets that empower individuals to shape their destinies.

Our journey continues with the understanding that each of us possesses the incredible potential to manifest our goals and desires. However, this art requires a blend of knowledge, intention, and disciplined practice. It is a path that beckons us to explore the intricate dance between our thoughts, emotions, and actions—a dance that has the power to sculpt our reality.

Within these pages, we will uncover a treasure trove of manifestation techniques and practices, each offering a unique path to awakening your latent abilities. These techniques, tried and tested by seekers and visionaries throughout history, are the keys to unlocking the door to your desires.

Visualization, the art of creating a vivid mental picture of your desired reality, will become your canvas on which dreams take shape. Affirmations will become the soundtrack resonating with positivity and purpose. Vision boards will serve as your visual compass, guiding you toward your aspirations.

But manifestation is not solely about the mind; it engages your entire being. Meditation and mindfulness will be your allies, grounding you in the present and aligning your energy with your intentions. Emotional alignment will teach you the art of feeling as if your goals are already achieved, a practice that sends ripples through the universe.

As we dive deeper, gratitude will become your daily ritual, attracting abundance and generating an unwavering belief in the possibility of your desires. Action steps will empower you to bridge the gap between thought and reality, while journaling will be your trusted companion on this life-long experience.

Manifestation is an art, but it is also a science—a harmonious blend of intention, action, and surrender. It requires both clarity of purpose and the release of attachment to outcomes. It beckons you to become the architect of your dreams and the captain of your destiny.

We will unravel the mysteries and intricacies of this art, offering practical guidance and exercises that will empower you to integrate these practices into your daily life. As you embrace the techniques and immerse yourself in the art of manifestation, you will witness the tangible, awe-inspiring results of your focused intention and aligned actions.

In prior chapters, we've underscored the significance of visualization in Chapter 3 and affirmed the power of affirmations in Chapter 5. However, it's crucial to recognize that these practices are not isolated but integral components of our manifestation techniques as well, which we'll revisit here for your convenience and further exploration. While you may already be acquainted with some of these methods, this compilation serves as a comprehensive catalog of diverse tools at your disposal.

These tools are your instruments for harnessing the power of manifestation, transforming your cherished goals and desires into tangible, lived experiences. Through the utilization of these techniques, you will embark on a journey that stretches the boundaries of what you once believed possible, expanding your horizons beyond the limits of imagination.

Visualization: Visualization is a powerful technique that involves mentally creating a detailed image of your desired outcome. By vividly imagining your goals as already achieved, you stimulate your subconscious mind to work towards making them a reality. This practice reinforces your belief in the attainability of your goals and aligns your thoughts with the desired outcome.

Affirmations: Affirmations are positive statements that reinforce your belief in achieving your goals. By repeating these affirmations regularly, you reprogram your subconscious mind to support your aspirations. When crafting affirmations, ensure they are present tense, positive, and specific to your goals. For example, "I am confident and successful in my career."

Vision Boards: Vision boards are visual representations of your goals and aspirations. You create a collage of images, words, and symbols that resonate with your desires and place it where you can see it regularly. Vision boards serve as constant reminders of your goals, keeping them in your awareness and reinforcing your commitment to achieving them.

Meditation and Mindfulness: Meditation and mindfulness practices help you stay present and focused on your goals. They reduce mental clutter and anxiety, allowing you to align your thoughts and emotions with your desires. Regular meditation builds clarity and concentration, enhancing your ability to manifest your goals effectively.

Emotional Alignment: Manifestation requires not only thinking positively but also feeling the emotions associated with your desired outcome. Emotional alignment involves generating the same feelings you would experience once your goal is achieved. This emotional resonance sends a powerful message to the universe and aligns your energy with your intentions.

Gratitude Practice: Expressing gratitude for what you have and for the manifestation of your goals is a powerful practice. Gratitude creates a positive mindset, attracts abundance, and reinforces the belief that your desires are attainable. Regularly acknowledging and appreciating your progress keeps you in a receptive state for further manifestation.

Action Steps: Manifestation is not solely about wishful thinking; it requires inspired action. Identify practical steps you can take to move closer to your goals. These action steps demonstrate your commitment and determination to bring your desires into reality.

Journaling: Keeping a manifestation journal helps you track your progress, document your experiences, and gain insights into your manifestation journey. Write down your goals, experiences, and any signs or synchronicities you encounter along the way. Journaling leads to self-reflection and keeps you motivated.

Release and Surrender: Sometimes, manifestation requires letting go of attachment to the outcome and trusting the timing. Release and surrender involve relinquishing control and having faith that your desires will manifest when the time is right.

These methods represent the most potent tools in the realm of positive thinking. The primary objective of this book is to equip you with foundational knowledge that can spark true changes in your life. In our pursuit of clarity and practicality, it's essential to acknowledge that many of these topics possess such depth that they could readily merit entire books of their own. However, our purpose here is to furnish you with actionable insights that demonstrate the remarkable potential of the human mind and the profound impact of maintaining a positive outlook on your life.

By adopting these practices, you can amplify your manifestation prowess, bringing your goals closer to becoming tangible realities.

Within the realm of positive thinking and manifestation, there exists a dynamic tool that has not yet been explored in these texts, the power of vision boards. Vision boards serve as a bridge between the ethereal realm of dreams and the tangible world of reality. In this section, we will explore the potential of vision boards, uncovering how they can assist you in turning your dreams and goals from mere thoughts into tangible manifestations.

Vision boards operate on the principles of visualization and the law of attraction. When you create a vision board, you immerse yourself in the positive emotions associated with your goals. This emotional engagement sends a powerful signal to your subconscious mind, which then seeks to align your actions with your desires.

The heart of a vision board lies in its images. Choose pictures that resonate with your goals and evoke strong emotions. These can be images of places you want to visit, people you admire, or achievements you aspire to. Use empowering statements that affirm your ability to achieve your desires.

Creating the Vision Board

Materials: Whether you choose a physical or digital vision board, you'll need materials such as magazines, scissors, glue, a poster board, or digital design software.

The Five-step Process of Visual Boards:

Set Your Intentions: Clarify your goals and intentions. What do you want to achieve or manifest in your life?

Gather Materials: Collect magazines, images, words, and symbols that align with your goals.

Design the Board: Arrange your chosen elements on a board or within a digital document. Be creative and intuitive in your layout.

Visualize It: Spend time with your vision board, allowing yourself to immerse in the feelings and emotions associated with your goals. Do not forget, Imagine them as already achieved.

Place Your Vision Board: Display your vision board where you can see it regularly. This serves as a constant reminder of your aspirations.

The potential benefits of vision boards are extensive and diverse, with countless individuals attesting to their extraordinary power and effectiveness. Exploring this phenomenon in greater depth will unveil a treasure trove of remarkable stories and experiences that range from the miraculous to the uncanny.

For instance, there are accounts of people dreaming about their ideal home, only to stumble upon their old vision board years later and realize they are living in the exact house they had placed on it. These personal anecdotes are both peculiar and profound, serving as a potent source of inspiration. They underscore the incredible influence of the mind within our universe, demonstrating that our aspirations are bound only by the limits of our imagination.

Benefits of the Board:

Clarity and Focus: Vision boards provide clarity about your goals and keep you focused on what truly matters.

Motivation: Regularly seeing your vision board can boost your motivation and determination to achieve your goals.

Positive Visualization: Engaging with your vision board encourages positive visualization, which is a powerful manifestation technique.

Alignment: As you align your thoughts and actions with your visualized goals, you create a powerful force for manifesting your desires.

Incorporating vision boards into your life can be a fun and effective way to manifest your dreams and goals. They serve as visual reminders of what you're working towards and help you stay motivated on your journey towards turning your dreams into reality.

8.3 Visualizing Your Goals

Visualization is a potent technique for manifesting your desires and making your goals more tangible and attainable. By vividly imagining your desired outcomes, you engage your subconscious mind and begin to create the mental and emotional framework necessary to turn those visions into reality. Here, we will explore the profound power of visualization and its role in helping you achieve your goals.

Visualization operates on the principle that your mind cannot distinguish between a vividly imagined scenario and a real-life experience. When you immerse yourself in a mental image of your goal, your brain responds as if you are actually experiencing it. This triggers the release of neurotransmitters associated with positive emotions and motivation, such as dopamine. As a result, you feel more motivated, focused, and confident in pursuing your goals.

This practice is not just a tool for goal setting; it can also help you overcome obstacles and challenges. By visualizing yourself confidently and resourcefully dealing with setbacks, you develop resilience and a positive mindset. This mental rehearsal prepares you to face challenges with determination and optimism, increasing your chances of success.

The practice of visualization extends beyond goal achievement. It can enhance various aspects of your life, including health, relationships, and personal growth. By incorporating visualization into your daily routine, you can boost your overall well-being and align your thoughts and actions with your aspirations. To harness the power of visualization effectively, you must practice it regularly.

The Five-Step Process of Visualization

Set Clear Goals: Begin by defining your goals with clarity. The more precise your vision, the more effectively you can visualize it.

Create a Quiet Space: Find a quiet and comfortable place where you can focus without distractions.

Relaxation: Start with deep breathing exercises or meditation to calm your mind and body.

Picture Your Goal: Close your eyes and create a mental image of your desired outcome. Imagine it in vivid detail, using all your senses. What do you see, hear, smell, taste, and feel in this imagined scenario?

Engage Emotion: Infuse your visualization with strong emotions. Feel the joy, excitement, and fulfillment as if you have already achieved your goal.

Practice this visualization daily, ideally in the morning or before bedtime, to reinforce your commitment and belief in your goals.

If you're new to the concept of vision boards or visualization, don't worry. Here, we've provided examples in three key areas of life where individuals commonly seek improvement or struggle. You can use these as templates or guidelines to better understand the process.

Example 1: Career Advancement

Identify Your Career Goals: Begin by clarifying your career aspirations. Determine the position you want to achieve, the skills you want to acquire, and the level of success you aim for.

Gather Visuals: Collect images and phrases that represent your career goals. These may include pictures of your dream workplace, successful professionals in your field, or symbols of achievement.

Layout and Design: Arrange your visuals on the board in an aesthetically pleasing manner. Consider organizing them by category, such as skills, achievements, and workplace environment.

Affirmations: Add affirmations related to your career goals. For example, "I am a confident and capable leader" or "I attract opportunities for career growth".

Visualization Routine: Set aside time each day to sit in front of your vision board. Close your eyes, visualize yourself in your desired career scenario, and feel the emotions associated with success.

Example 2: Health and Fitness

Define Your Health Goals: Determine your health and fitness objectives, whether it's losing weight, getting in shape, or adopting a healthier lifestyle.

Find Visual Aids: Collect images that represent your health goals. These may include pictures of fit individuals, healthy meals, exercise equipment, or serene natural settings for relaxation.

Layout and Organization: Arrange the visuals on your board in a way that motivates and inspires you. Consider incorporating sections for exercise routines, meal plans, and wellness practices.

Affirmations: Include affirmations that reinforce your commitment to health, such as "I prioritize my well-being" or "I make healthy choices every day."

Daily Ritual: Spend a few moments each day standing in front of your vision board. Visualize yourself embodying the healthy lifestyle you desire and experience the positive emotions associated with it.

Example 3: Personal Growth

Reflect on Your Growth: Think about the areas in which you wish to grow personally. It could be building confidence, cultivating resilience, or enhancing your creativity.

Visual Inspirations: Find visuals that resonate with your personal growth aspirations. These might include images of confident individuals, books, quotes, or symbols of personal development.

Board Design: Organize your visuals on the board in a way that inspires and motivates you. Create sections for specific areas of personal growth, such as self-confidence or creativity.

Positive Affirmations: Incorporate affirmations that align with your personal growth journey. For example, "I believe in myself and my abilities" or "I embrace challenges as opportunities for growth."

Daily Connection: Dedicate a few minutes each day to stand in front of your vision board. Close your eyes, visualize yourself embodying the qualities you aspire to, and feel the power of personal growth.

Harnessing the incredible power of visualization, will lead to a new level of self-discovery and transformation. You've learned that your mind is a gateway to limitless possibilities, and that by vividly imagining your goals, you activate the forces of creation within you. As you continue to practice visualization, remember that consistency is key. Make it a daily habit to immerse yourself in the mental images of your desires, nurturing your dreams with unwavering faith.

But the power of visualization doesn't stop at personal goals. It extends to every facet of your life, enriching your health, relationships, and personal growth. It's a tool that empowers you to cultivate resilience and a positive mindset, enabling you to conquer challenges and setbacks with grace and determination.

Remember that you possess the ability to transform your life. The vision board is a tangible tool you have to manifest your dreams. With every image and affirmation, you're sending a powerful message to the universe, now watch as it conspires to turn your dreams into reality.

Chapter 9: Embracing Abundance and Gratitude

9.1 The Abundance Mindset

In all of human existence, there exists a spectrum of mindsets that shape the way we perceive the world. At one end, some view life through the lens of scarcity, believing that resources, opportunities, and success are limited. They constantly worry about what they lack and fear they'll never have enough. This scarcity mindset leads to anxiety, competition, and a sense of deprivation.

At the opposite end of the spectrum lies a perspective known as the 'Abundance Mindset.' This mindset is a profound shift in consciousness that beckons us to embrace the limitless possibilities that life offers. It is the belief that the universe is abundant, generous, and overflowing with opportunities, waiting for us to claim them.

The abundance mindset is not a mere positivity exercise or a shallow affirmation. It's a fundamental shift in our perception of reality. It invites us to recognize that abundance isn't solely about material wealth, but an expansive outlook that encompasses love, joy, creativity, and all the intangible rewards life has to offer. It's about seeing the world as a place of boundless potential, where success and fulfillment are not scarce commodities reserved for a select few, but readily available to all who dare to believe.

Central to the abundance mindset is the concept that there is enough to go around for everyone. It collaborates, cooperates, and has a sense of interconnectedness with others. It frees us from the shackles of envy and comparison, as we come to understand that someone else's success doesn't diminish our own possibilities.

Embracing the abundance mindset is not about denying the existence of challenges or hardships. Instead, it's about changing our response to them. When faced with setbacks, those with an abundance mindset view them as opportunities for growth and learning, rather than insurmountable obstacles.

In this chapter, we will look at the philosophy behind abundance and explore practical ways to use this mindset. By the end, you'll be equipped with the tools to embrace abundance in all its forms, ushering in a life of greater joy, fulfillment, and gratitude.

The Abundance Mindset can be deconstructed into

several key aspects, each of which collaboratively shapes your perspective on life. By focusing on these components, you can gain a deeper understanding of their significance and gather valuable insights to apply them effectively in your own context.

Belief in Unlimited Possibility: The abundance mindset is grounded in the belief that opportunities, resources, and success are limitless. Instead of dwelling on scarcity and limitations, individuals with this mindset recognize that there's an abundance of possibilities waiting to be explored. They approach life with a sense of optimism and curiosity, expecting that the universe has much to offer.

Gratitude in the Present Moment: People with an abundance mindset appreciate what they have in the present moment. They are not constantly yearning for more or dwelling on what they lack. Instead, they cultivate gratitude for their current circumstances, recognizing the richness of their experiences, relationships, and possessions.

Embrace Challenges: Rather than fearing challenges and setbacks, those with an abundance mindset view them as opportunities for growth and learning. They understand that obstacles are a natural part of life's journey and believe that they have the inner resources to overcome them. Challenges are seen as stepping stones toward personal development and success.

Open to Collaboration: Individuals with an abundance mindset are open to collaboration and cooperation with others. They don't see success as a finite resource that must be guarded or competed for. Instead, they believe that there's enough success to be shared and that helping others achieve their goals can lead to mutual prosperity.

Positive Self-Image: This mindset is closely tied to a positive self-image. People who embrace abundance see themselves as capable, deserving, and empowered to create the life they desire. They don't let self-doubt or limiting beliefs hold them back. Instead, they trust in their abilities and value their worthiness.

Focus on Solutions: When faced with challenges or problems, those with an abundance mindset focus on finding solutions rather than dwelling on the issues. They maintain a proactive and problem-solving attitude, believing that there's always a way to overcome obstacles and move forward.

Abundance in All Areas: The abundance mindset isn't limited to material wealth. It encompasses all aspects of life, including love, happiness, creativity, and fulfillment. People with this mindset seek to experience abundance in every area of their lives, recognizing that true richness extends beyond monetary wealth.

Giving Back: Those with an abundance mindset often feel a desire to give back and contribute to the well-being of others. They understand that their success can be a source of inspiration and support for others on their journeys. This leads to acts of kindness, generosity, and a sense of purpose.

Cultivating the abundance mindset is a multifaceted journey that involves a profound shift in one's perspective, the intentional reframing of limiting beliefs, and a wholehearted embrace of the idea that the universe is inherently abundant and poised to support our deepest goals and aspirations.

It is a formidable mindset, one that has the potential to usher in a heightened sense of joy, unwavering resilience in the face of adversity, and an unparalleled sense of fulfillment across all spheres of life.

Now that we know what the abundant mindset is, we can learn to use it to our advantage and alter our previous or negative perspective we may have entertained. Shifting from a perspective of scarcity to one of abundance is a process that requires intentional effort and a commitment to change.

The first step in adopting an abundance mindset is becoming aware of your current thought patterns. Take time to reflect on your beliefs and attitudes about abundance, success, and prosperity. Are you often focused on what you lack or what you have? Are you prone to negative self-talk or self-limiting beliefs? Acknowledging these patterns is first.

Once you've identified your limiting beliefs, challenge them. Ask yourself if they are based on facts or if they are simply ingrained thought patterns. For example, if you believe that opportunities are scarce, try to find evidence to the contrary. Seek out stories of people who have achieved success in your field or area of interest. Make a daily habit of listing things you are grateful for. This practice helps you focus on the abundance that already exists in your life, no matter how small or seemingly insignificant. You may also create a mental image of the life you desire, filled with prosperity, opportunities, and happiness. Immerse yourself in this visualization regularly to reinforce the feeling of abundance. Positive affirmations can also counteract negative thought patterns. Develop a list of affirmations that emphasize abundance and success. Repeat them daily to rewire your subconscious mind.

Seeking out positive influences, whether through books, podcasts, or relationships can also be very beneficial. Surrounding yourself with abundance-oriented individuals and resources can reinforce your new mindset. It isn't just about thinking positively; it's also about taking proactive steps toward your goals. Break down your aspirations into actionable steps and work consistently toward them. Each small success reinforces your belief in abundance.

Understand that setbacks are a part of life. Instead of viewing them as failures, see them as opportunities for growth. Embrace challenges as chances to learn and improve. Ultimately, celebrate your achievements, no matter how minor they may seem. Recognizing your successes, both big and small, reinforces the idea that abundance is attainable.

Shifting from a scarcity mindset to an abundance mindset is a process that takes time. Be patient with yourself and allow the transformation to unfold gradually. By following these steps and consistently working on your mindset, you can make a significant shift from scarcity to abundance thinking, opening the door to a more fulfilling and prosperous life.

Transitioning from understanding the abundance mindset, we now look into a critical aspect of putting this mindset into action: recognizing opportunities and possibilities. The abundance mindset sets the stage for us to approach life with a positive and open outlook, believing that there are endless opportunities waiting to be discovered. In this section, we will explore practical strategies and mindsets that can help you spot opportunities, make the most of them, and ultimately lead a more fulfilling and successful life. Just as the abundance mindset can reshape your perspective on the world, the ability to identify opportunities can open doors to new horizons and uncharted possibilities.

To begin recognizing opportunities and possibilities is to remain open to new experiences and ideas. Embrace a mindset that is receptive to change and willing to explore the unknown. Sometimes, opportunities may come from unexpected sources.

Continuous learning and personal growth are essential for recognizing opportunities. Stay curious and invest in your education and skills. The more you know, the better equipped you'll be to identify opportunities that align with your interests and abilities.

Constructing a diverse network of contacts can lead to new opportunities. Attend networking events, connect with professionals in your field, and engage with people from different backgrounds. Often, opportunities arise through personal and professional connections.

Remember to keep up with industry trends, market developments, and current events. Being informed about what's happening in the world can help you spot opportunities before others do. Subscribe to relevant publications, follow industry blogs, and participate in discussions. Creativity is a powerful tool for recognizing possibilities. Expand your creative thinking by exploring different perspectives and brainstorming ideas. Challenge conventional thinking and look for innovative solutions to problems.

Practice mindfulness to stay present in the moment. When you're fully engaged in the present, you're more likely to notice these opportunities as they arise. Mindfulness also helps you make conscious choices and decisions. Recognizing opportunities often involves taking calculated risks. Don't be afraid to step out of your comfort zone when you see a potential opportunity. Assess the risks and benefits, and be prepared to take action.

Even if you venture beyond your comfort zone and encounter setbacks or failures, these experiences are valuable lessons gained in your pursuit. Rather than avoiding challenges altogether, facing them head-on provides an opportunity for growth and learning. setbacks or failures, in this context, should not be viewed as inherently negative; instead, they are stepping stones on your journey toward success.

Maintaining a positive attitude is essential for recognizing opportunities. A negative mindset can blind you to possibilities. Stay optimistic and believe in your ability to create opportunities. By incorporating these strategies into your life, you can become more adept at recognizing opportunities and possibilities, which is a key element of the abundance mindset. This shift in perspective can lead to greater success and fulfillment in various aspects of life.

Remember that the abundance mindset is an ongoing process, and it requires consistent practice and self-awareness. As you continue your exploration of this mindset, you'll discover that the more you give thanks for the abundance in your life, the more abundance you attract. It's a beautiful cycle that can lead to a life filled with joy, fulfillment, and a deep sense of gratitude for all that you have and all that is yet to come.

In the next section, we will go deeper into the practice of gratitude and how it can become a cornerstone of your daily life. Exploring the ever-changing effects of living with gratitude and how it can amplify the abundance mindset, bringing you even closer to your goals and dreams.

9.2 The Gratitude Lifestyle

A deep sense of gratitude can profoundly impact your life, your relationships, and your overall well-being. Gratitude is more than just a fleeting feeling of thankfulness; it's a way of living and perceiving the world around you. It's about recognizing and appreciating the abundance that exists in your life, no matter how big or small.

We briefly introduced the concept of the gratitude habit in Chapter 3. Now, let's look over these principles and examine how they align with embracing the gratitude lifestyle.

The gratitude lifestyle is a conscious choice to view every moment as an opportunity for gratitude, to seek out the silver linings in every situation, and to express your appreciation regularly. It's a mindset that can lead to a more positive, joyful, and fulfilling existence. So, if you're ready to elevate your life to new heights, let's discuss the world of gratitude and discover the incredible benefits it has to offer.

Starting with the science behind gratitude, its profound effects on your mental and physical health, and practical techniques for incorporating gratitude into your daily routine, let us explore the ways in which gratitude can enhance your relationships, boost your happiness, and help you navigate life's challenges with grace and resilience. Whether you're new to the concept or have already begun using it, there are valuable insights and actionable steps to embrace the gratitude lifestyle fully.

Keep an open heart and a curious spirit. The gratitude lifestyle has the power to shift your perspective and illuminate the beauty and abundance that surround you. It's a path that can lead you to a life filled with appreciation, contentment, and an ever-deepening sense of gratitude for the wondrous gift of existence.

Embracing the Gratitude Lifestyle

One of the most effective ways to incorporate gratitude into your daily life is by maintaining a gratitude journal. Each day, take a few moments to write down three to five things you're thankful for. These can be as simple as a beautiful sunset, a warm cup of tea, or a kind gesture from a friend.

Don't just feel gratitude; express it. Take the time to tell the people in your life how much you appreciate them and their actions. A heartfelt "thank you" can go a long way in strengthening your relationships. Throughout the day, pause and mindfully appreciate the small things around you.

It could be the taste of your morning coffee, the feel of sunshine on your skin, or the sound of birds chirping. Being present in these moments amplifies your sense of gratitude. Instead of dwelling on what you lack or desire, focus on what you already possess and cherish. This shift from "want" to "have" can lead to a more content and fulfilled life.

Incorporate gratitude into your meditation practice. Spend a few minutes meditating on the things you're grateful for, allowing the positive emotions associated with gratitude to wash over you. Extend your gratitude by performing acts of kindness. Helping others not only benefits them but also reinforces your sense of appreciation for your ability to make a positive impact.

Aspects of the Gratitude Lifestyle

Relationships: In your interactions with loved ones, express gratitude for their presence in your life. Share specific reasons why you appreciate them.

Example: Imagine you have a close friend who's been supportive during a difficult time in your life. Instead of taking this for granted, you express your gratitude by writing a heartfelt letter or simply telling them how much their support has meant to you. Your friend feels appreciated, and your bond strengthens.

Career: In your workplace, acknowledge the efforts and contributions of colleagues and coworkers. Recognizing their hard work can create a more positive and collaborative environment.

Example: At work, you notice a colleague who consistently goes the extra mile to help the team. You express your gratitude by publicly acknowledging their efforts during a team meeting. This recognition boosts their morale, encourages their continued dedication, and creates a more positive work atmosphere.

Health: Embrace a sense of gratitude for your health, regardless of its current state. Taking care of your body becomes an act of self-love and appreciation.

Example: Suppose you've recently recovered from an illness. Instead of dwelling on the challenges you faced, you focus on gratitude for your returning health.

You make a conscious effort to nourish your body with healthy food, regular exercise, and adequate rest, all with a sense of appreciation for your well-being.

Challenges: Even in challenging times, find reasons to be grateful. These experiences often come with valuable lessons and opportunities for growth.

Let's say you encounter a setback in your career, a project you have been working on doesn't succeed as expected. Instead of dwelling on the failure, you reflect on the lessons learned. You express gratitude for the opportunity to grow and adapt, realizing that these challenges have the potential to lead to future success.

Incorporating the gratitude lifestyle into your daily routine can transform the way you perceive and interact with the world around you. It's not just about saying 'thank you' occasionally; it's about embracing a deeper sense of appreciation for the people, experiences, and opportunities that enrich your life.

By regularly practicing gratitude, you will find that positivity becomes a natural part of your existence. You'll notice more moments of joy and contentment, even in the midst of challenges. The effect of your gratitude will touch the lives of those you encounter, strengthening your relationships and creating a more harmonious environment.

As you embark on this new lifestyle, remember that it's not about denying the existence of difficulties or hardships but rather about choosing to focus on the blessings that exist alongside them. This is a path to a more fulfilling, positive, and joyful life. It's a reminder that no matter the circumstances, there is always something to be thankful for.

With the adoption of the gratitude lifestyle, you can enhance your overall well-being, develop deeper connections with others, and navigate life's ups and downs with a resilient and positive mindset.

9.3 Acts of Kindness

Acts of kindness are a powerful tool in generating positive thinking and creating a positive effect in your life. These acts go beyond mere politeness or social etiquette; they are intentional gestures of goodwill and compassion towards others. Kindness not only benefits those on the receiving end but also has a profound impact on your own mindset and overall well-being.

In the context of this book, kindness is a cornerstone of maintaining a positive mindset. It aligns with the abundance mindset, as it acknowledges that there is enough goodness to go around and that sharing positivity only multiplies it. Acts of kindness also reinforce the gratitude lifestyle, as they invite you to appreciate the opportunities you have to make a difference in someone's life.

Kindness strengthens your relationships, making it an essential component of positive relationships, which we explored in Chapter 7. Effective communication, empathy, and understanding, which we discussed in that chapter, are all deeply intertwined with acts of kindness. By practicing kindness, you actively contribute to creating more harmonious and supportive relationships.

Now, let's provide some real-world examples of acts of kindness to illustrate its practical application:

Random Acts of Kindness: These are the small unexpected acts like paying for a stranger's coffee, leaving an uplifting note for a coworker, or complimenting a passerby that can brighten someone's day and infuse positivity into your own.

Volunteer Work: Dedicate your time to a cause you're passionate about. Whether it's volunteering at a local shelter, participating in a community cleanup, or mentoring a young student, giving back generates a sense of fulfillment and reinforces positive values.

Helping Others: Offering assistance to someone in need, whether it's helping an elderly neighbor with chores or supporting a friend during a tough time, strengthens bonds and creates a culture of support.

Acts of Generosity: Sharing your resources, such as donating to a charity, contributing to a crowdfunding campaign, or giving away unused items, not only helps others but also reminds you of the abundance in your life.

Listening Actively: Sometimes, the most significant act of kindness is simply being present and actively listening to someone who needs to be heard. Showing empathy and understanding can have a profound impact on their well-being and your own sense of connection.

These examples showcase how acts of kindness are woven into various aspects of life, from personal growth to nurturing positive relationships and embodying the principles discussed in your book.

Kindness extends its reach into self-improvement, emphasizing that personal growth doesn't occur in isolation. It thrives in a climate of compassion. When you engage in acts of kindness, you not only uplift others but also reinforce your commitment to positive thinking. The act of kindness displays the idea that your path to self-improvement isn't solitary; it's a collective journey where the seeds of positivity are sown not just within yourself, but also within the hearts of those around you.

Chapter 10: Living a Positively Empowered Lifestyle

10.1 Integrating Positive Thinking

In the final chapter of this transformative adventure, we go deep into the heart of what it means to live a positively empowered life. It's more than just adopting a few positive thinking techniques; it's about embracing a holistic positive thinking lifestyle that permeates every aspect of your existence. The significance of this integration cannot be overstated, for it's the key to unlocking lasting joy, resilience, and fulfillment.

As we explore the components of this holistic approach, you'll discover that positive thinking isn't merely a tool to wield in moments of uncertainty, it becomes your way of life, your guiding light through the twists and turns of your unique journey. Let's embark on this final leg of our voyage, where we will learn to not only embrace positivity but also sustain it for the long haul, navigating life's challenges with unwavering optimism.

To do this we must learn to embrace a holistic positive thinking lifestyle and most importantly maintain it in life. No matter how painful or frustrating life can often seem, the universe is most definitely still on your side; However, that doesn't mean it won't throw you a curve ball or two. Let's break down the process to integrate this style of living and maintain it on a day to day basis for the various aspects of our lives.

Positive thinking should not exist in isolation but rather seamlessly blend into all aspects of life. It's not just a mental exercise; it's a way of approaching and experiencing the world. Here is how we integrate positive thinking and how it can influence each area in life:

Personal Growth

Self-Improvement: Positivity fuels a desire for continuous self-improvement. When you view challenges as opportunities for growth, you actively seek to expand your knowledge, skills, and experiences.

Resilience: A positive mindset enhances your resilience. In the face of setbacks, you maintain the belief that you can overcome adversity, making you more likely to persevere and achieve your goals.

Relationships

Effective Communication: Positivity builds effective communication by promoting active listening, empathy, and understanding. It enables you to connect more deeply with others and resolve conflicts constructively.

Nurturing Bonds: Positive individuals tend to build stronger, more harmonious relationships. They radiate warmth and kindness, attracting like-minded individuals who appreciate their uplifting presence.

Work and Career

Productivity: A positive mindset enhances productivity and creativity. It encourages a can-do attitude, leading to innovative solutions and improved job performance.

Leadership: Positive individuals often make effective leaders. Their optimism and ability to inspire others can lead to team success and a more positive work environment.

Health and Well-Being

Stress Reduction: Positivity helps reduce stress by allowing a sense of calm and control. It can lower cortisol levels, leading to better physical and mental health.

Lifestyle Choices: Positive individuals are more likely to make healthy lifestyle choices, such as eating well, exercising regularly, and getting enough sleep. These habits contribute to overall well-being.

Overall Well-Being

Contentment: Positivity is linked to greater life satisfaction. When you focus on the positive aspects of life, you experience more contentment and joy.

Optimism: Positivity breeds optimism about the future. You develop a sense of hope and belief that better days lie ahead, which can positively impact your overall well-being.

A holistic positive thinking lifestyle is vital because it shapes the quality of your life and influences the lives of those around you. It empowers you to overcome challenges with resilience, make decisions aligned with your values, and keep fulfilling relationships. Moreover, it creates a ripple effect, spreading positivity and making the world a better place.

By embracing positivity as a way of life, you not only enhance your well-being but also become a beacon of inspiration and hope for others on their journey towards a more positive and empowered existence.

An essential habit for sustaining this lifestyle involves consistently monitoring your advancement and commemorating your accomplishments, regardless of their scale. No matter the magnitude of your progress or the significance of your achievement, it's critical to reward yourself and keep a record of it, whether you prefer traditional pen-and-paper methods or digital tracking. This practice is vital for staying committed to the holistic positive thinking lifestyle.

Tracking progress helps you stay motivated and maintain momentum. When you see tangible evidence of your achievements, you're more likely to stay committed to your goals. Then, celebrating these small victories boosts your confidence and self-esteem. Each success, no matter how small, reinforces your belief in your abilities, making you more adept in overcoming challenges. Some simple strategies for this include:

Set Milestones: Break your long-term goals into smaller, manageable ones. Tracking progress becomes more accessible when you have clear checkpoints along the way.

Use Visual Aids: Visual aids like charts, graphs, or journals can help you visually track your progress. Seeing your journey on paper reinforces your commitment.

Regularly Reflecting: Take time to reflect regularly on your accomplishments, no matter how minor. This practice helps you stay connected to your goals and the progress you've made.

Celebrating Your Wins: Don't wait for significant milestones to celebrate. Celebrate even the smallest victories whether it's completing a task, finishing a personal best, or making progress toward your goals.

Sharing Achievements: Share your successes with friends or family. Sharing these achievements with others not only strengthens your support network but also reinforces your sense of accomplishment.

Rewarding Yourself: Treat yourself when you achieve a milestone. Rewards can be simple, like a favorite meal or a leisurely activity you enjoy.

Learning: If you encounter setbacks, view them as opportunities for growth rather than failures. Analyze what went wrong, adjust your approach, and continue forward.

By weaving these strategies into your daily routine, you establish the seamless integration of tracking progress and reveling in success as indispensable components of your positive and empowered lifestyle. As you've learned from earlier chapters, monitoring your progress not only boosts the release of neurotransmitters associated with positive emotions but also reinforces the reward system in your brain, motivating you to achieve more.

Moreover, regularly celebrating your achievements, no matter how small, contributes to a sense of fulfillment and reinforces the positive feedback loop of positivity, ensuring that positivity becomes an intrinsic part of your life that can also spread to others.

The concept of the ripple effect is an amazing and profound manifestation of the power of positivity. It illustrates how one person's positive thoughts, actions, and energy can create a chain reaction, spreading positivity far and wide. Understanding and harnessing the ripple effect is a key aspect of living positively.

The ripple effect is often associated with the "butterfly effect," a term coined in chaos theory. It suggests that a small change in one part of a complex system can lead to significant and unpredictable changes elsewhere. In the context of this book, and of positive thinking and actions, this means that even our smallest acts of kindness or moments of positivity can have far-reaching consequences. Positivity spreads through various mechanisms.

When people witness acts of kindness or experience positive energy from others, they often feel inspired to pass it on. This inspiration can lead to a cascade of positive actions. As we have seen earlier, emotions are contagious. When we interact with someone who radiates positivity, we tend to absorb some of that positivity ourselves. This, in turn, influences how we interact with others.

Positive behavior can set social norms and expectations. When someone consistently exhibits positive actions, it can encourage others to do the same. There is often the term, "Pay It Forward". The idea of paying it forward is a practical example of the ripple effect. When someone receives a kindness or favor, they may feel compelled to do something kind for someone else, creating a continuous chain of positivity.

The ripple effect can be caused by random acts of kindness, social media, volunteering or engaging in community projects, or even a leader in the workplace demonstrating his extensive understanding and use of a positive thinking mindset.

Understanding the ripple effect is significant for leading a life of endless positive change. It highlights that our efforts to generate this positivity and make positive choices have a broader impact on the world than we may realize. By consciously choosing positivity and spreading kindness, we contribute to a more compassionate, harmonious, and uplifting world.

Sustaining Positivity in the Long Term

To truly embrace and benefit from the principles discussed in this book, you must grow a sustainable positive mindset and lifestyle. This brief sub-section explores the significance of sustaining positivity in the long term, offering insights and strategies to ensure that your journey remains fulfilling and enduring.

Sustaining positivity over time can present unique challenges. Life is filled with ups and downs, and maintaining a positive outlook during difficult moments can be particularly challenging. Nevertheless, it's precisely during these challenging times that the benefits of long-term positivity become most apparent. Here's three key points to navigate these challenges:

Resilience: Long-term positivity involves developing resilience. Resilience enables you to bounce back from setbacks, adapt to change, and maintain a positive outlook even in the face of adversity.

Mindfulness: Mindfulness practices, as discussed in earlier chapters, play a crucial role in sustaining positivity. By staying present and fully experiencing each moment, you can find joy and contentment in everyday life, regardless of external circumstances.

Self-Compassion: Be kind to yourself always. Recognize that setbacks and negative emotions are a natural part of life. Practice self-compassion by treating yourself with the same kindness and understanding that you extend to others.

In light of these three principles, it becomes imperative for us to consistently reinforce the positive thinking processes we have acquired and to perpetuate the application of these techniques and strategies for sustained success in our endeavors, not only in the present but also well into the future. Below, we will recap six practical and easy-to-follow methods that can serve as a blueprint for continual success.

Six Simple Strategies for Long Term Success

Daily Habits: Create daily habits that reinforce positivity, such as gratitude journaling, meditation, or affirmations. Consistency is key to making these practices a natural part of your life.

Goal-setting: Continue setting and pursuing meaningful goals. Goals give you a sense of purpose and direction, helping you stay motivated and focused on positive outcomes.

Social Support: Surround yourself with positive individuals. Maintain healthy relationships that uplift and inspire you. Your social circle plays a significant role in sustaining positivity.

Adaptability: Embrace change and uncertainty as opportunities for growth. View challenges as learning experiences, and remain adaptable in the face of adversity.

Self-Care: Prioritize self-care to maintain physical and mental well-being. Exercise, a balanced diet, and adequate sleep contribute to your overall positivity.

Continued Learning: Keep learning and expanding your knowledge. Curiosity and personal growth contribute to a sense of fulfillment and positivity.

10.2 Your Positive Future

As we embark on the final chapter of our travels, it's essential to pause and reflect on the voyage we've taken together. Throughout these pages, we've explored the profound and enduring power of positive thinking, diving deep into the science, psychology, and practical applications that make it a force to be reckoned with. We've unearthed the impressive power of mindfulness, gratitude, and visualization, using them as our guiding stars towards a brighter, more purposeful life.

With every chapter, we've equipped ourselves with precious tools, from the art of affirmations to the resilience needed to overcome life's challenges. We have viewed the intricacies of our relationships, discovering how they can be transformed through positivity. We have opened our hearts to abundance and embraced the lifestyle of gratitude. Acts of kindness have become our daily companions, creating ripples of positivity that touch every corner of our world. We have learned not just to think positively but to live it.

We carry with us the accumulated wisdom, hope, and determination that we have found in positive thinking. We recognize that it doesn't end here; rather, it unfolds into an exciting and limitless future where positivity continues to guide our steps.

As we stand on the edge of concluding our shared odyssey through the realms of positive thinking, it is a profound moment to pause, breathe, and reflect. Your journey through these chapters has been a personal and transformative one. You have looked into the depths of your mind, challenging old thought patterns, and discovering the incredible potential that positivity unlocks.

Take a moment to acknowledge the progress you've made or things you may have learned. Perhaps with curiosity or a yearning for change that you decided to pick up this book. Now, think of how you have embraced the principles of positive thinking, making them a part of your daily life. Recall the challenges you may have faced and overcome, the moments of clarity and insight that have illuminated your path.

This demonstrates your commitment to growth, resilience, and the belief that positivity is not just a concept but a living, breathing force within you. You have harnessed its power to reshape your mindset, relationships, and even your future. The lessons learned and the practices adopted have transformed you in subtle yet profound ways.

As you reflect more on your journey, know that this is not the end but a continuation. The seeds of positivity you have sown are destined to bear fruit in the days, months, and years to come. Your story is still being written, and the chapters ahead hold the promise of even greater self-discovery, growth, and fulfillment.

Celebrate the insights gained and the positive changes you've initiated. Carry this reflection with you as a reminder of your inner strength and the boundless potential that positivity has unlocked within you.

In these pages, we've passed through profound landscapes of positive thinking, exploring its depths and discovering its limitless potential. As we approach the culmination of our adventure, it's time to distill the essence of our shared experience.

Let this small tome serve as a reminder that our thoughts possess the power to shape our reality, influence our choices, and chart the course of our destinies. Through the chapters and insights, you've witnessed the potential of positive thinking.

You may have learned that positivity is not merely a fleeting emotion but a way of life, a mindset that empowers you to overcome challenges, nurture meaningful relationships, and pursue your dreams with unwavering belief. It's a force that transcends the boundaries of circumstance, providing a beacon of light in even the darkest of moments.

As you close this chapter of our journey, carry with you the knowledge that the journey of positive thinking is ongoing. It is a path you will continue to walk, armed with the wisdom and tools you have gathered along the way. Your life is a canvas, and positive thinking is the vibrant palette with which you paint your future.

Remember that positivity is not a destination but a companion, guiding you through the complexities of existence. It's a choice you make each day, a way in which you view the world, and a force that propels you toward a brighter and more fulfilling tomorrow.

May the principles and practices shared here serve you on your path. May you continue to harness the power of positive thinking to shape a life filled with joy, purpose, and boundless potential. Your journey is far from over, and your positive future awaits, ready to be embraced with open arms and an open heart.

I want to express my deepest gratitude for selecting my book as your trusted guide on your interest in positive thinking. This book was crafted with a deliberate focus on providing you with a concise, yet all-encompassing guide to this powerful mindset. At the end of this book I will provide easy to access pages of the key methods or techniques you may use for convenience.

As you hold this resource in your hands, consider making it a constant presence on your desk or within your chosen space, wherever you do your reading or deep thinking. Feel free to highlight, use sticky notes, or underline the passages that truly resonate with you, reinforcing the fundamental concepts that you are drawn to, these may provide the most noticeable change.

"The Universe Has Your Back" is a small book of inspiration designed to be readily accessible whenever you seek information or guidance on your path of positivity. Remember, the universe has your back, and this book is here to remind you of the unwavering support and boundless potential it holds for your life.

About The Author

The realm of positive thinking is profoundly vast, encompassing a multitude of subjects, some of which I may not have gone into here. My focus has been on the concepts that have personally resonated with me and proven effective in my life.

I have explored countless self-help books on positive thinking. My acknowledgments extend to all the authors throughout the centuries whose profound insights have aided my understanding of this field. Their diligent research paved the way for me to unearth all the knowledge I have placed into this concise and accessible volume.

This book is actually a first for me as an author, and I am aware that it most likely has imperfections and room for refinement. Nevertheless, my primary goal has been to share the most valuable insights into these pages, striking a balance between information and brevity.

I express my sincere gratitude for choosing this book. I apologize for the formatting of the text on the pages I was having difficulties with; however, I am hoping it still serves to get the information to you. I welcome constructive feedback and hope that it has provided you with some measure of assistance and inspiration. Once again, thank you for your support.

Mindfulness Techniques

1. Mindful Breathing

One of the simplest yet most effective mindfulness practices is mindful breathing. Find a quiet place, sit comfortably, and focus your attention on your breath. Inhale deeply through your nose, feeling the air fill your lungs, and exhale slowly through your mouth. Pay attention to the sensation of each breath, the rise and fall of your chest, and the rhythmic flow of air. If your mind wanders, gently bring your focus back to your breath. This practice can be done for a few minutes anytime during your day to center yourself and reduce stress.

2. Body Scan Meditation

Body scan meditation is a technique that involves systematically scanning your body from head to toe with focused attention. Start by bringing your awareness to the top of your head and slowly move it down, noticing any sensations, tension, or discomfort. This practice helps you become more attuned to physical sensations and promotes relaxation. It's particularly helpful in releasing tension and promoting positive feelings.

3. Mindful Walking

Transform your daily walk into a mindfulness practice. As you walk, pay attention to the sensation of each step, the feeling of your feet connecting with the ground, and the movement of your body. Engage your senses—notice the sights, sounds, and smells around you. By staying present during your walk, you can turn it into a calming and rejuvenating experience.

4. Gratitude Journaling

Each day, take a few moments to write down things you are grateful for in a gratitude journal. This practice shifts your focus to positive aspects of your life and encourages you to savor and appreciate them. Gratitude journaling leads to a positive outlook and reminds you of the abundance in your life.

5. Mindful Eating

Mindful eating involves savoring each bite of your meals with full awareness. Pay attention to the flavors, textures, and aromas of your food. Chew slowly and appreciate the nourishment it provides. Avoid distractions like screens or rushing through meals. Mindful eating not only enhances your enjoyment of food but also promotes mindful living.

6. Three-Minute Breathing Space

The three-minute breathing space is a brief mindfulness practice you can do anytime, anywhere. It consists of three steps:

Step 1 (Awareness): Take a minute to become aware of your thoughts, emotions, and bodily sensations. Acknowledge whatever is present without judgment.

Step 2 (Gathering): In the next minute, focus your attention on your breath. Take a few deep breaths, centering yourself in the present moment.

Step 3 (Expanding): In the final minute, expand your awareness to your entire body and surroundings. Notice the bigger picture and a sense of spaciousness.

7. Mindful Use of Technology

In our digital age, it's essential to practice mindful technology use. Set aside specific times to check emails, social media, or screens. During these periods, be fully present with your digital tasks. When not using technology, unplug and engage in offline activities mindfully.

8. Loving-Kindness Meditation

Loving-kindness meditation, also known as "metta" meditation, is a practice of sending love and well-wishes to yourself and others. Begin by directing loving-kindness to yourself, then to loved ones, acquaintances, and even those you may have conflicts with. This practice leads to compassion, empathy, and positivity toward yourself and others.

9. Mindful Conversations

Practice mindful listening during conversations. Instead of planning your response or judgment, truly listen to the speaker. Pay attention to their words, tone, and emotions. Respond with empathy and kindness, fostering positive and meaningful interactions.

10. Daily Reflection

End your day with a brief period of reflection. Consider the positive moments, accomplishments, and acts of kindness you experienced during the day. Reflect on how these moments made you feel and express gratitude for them. This practice encourages positive self-reflection and reinforces positivity.

Gratitude Techniques

Gratitude Journaling: Set aside a few minutes each day to write down three things you are grateful for. These can be simple pleasures, moments of kindness, or positive experiences. Reflect on why you appreciate them.

Morning Gratitude: Start your day by expressing gratitude. As you wake up, think of one thing you are grateful for. It could be the warmth of the sun, a cozy bed, or the prospect of a new day.

Three Good Things: Before going to bed, recall three good things that happened during the day. Reflect on why they made you feel grateful and appreciative.

The Gratitude Walk: Take a mindful walk in nature or around your neighborhood. As you walk, focus on the beauty around you—the colors of flowers, the sound of birds, or the feeling of fresh air. Express gratitude for the natural world.

Gratitude Affirmations: Create gratitude affirmations that resonate with you. For example, "I am grateful for the abundance in my life" or "I appreciate the love and support of my family." Repeat these affirmations throughout the day.

Mealtime Gratitude: Before each meal, take a moment to express gratitude for the food you are about to enjoy. Consider the journey of the food from its source to your plate and appreciate it fully.

The Gratitude Jar: Keep a gratitude jar or box. Whenever something makes you feel grateful, write it down on a slip of paper and put it in the jar. Over time, you'll have a collection of positive moments to revisit.

Gratitude Meditation: Dedicate a few minutes to a gratitude meditation. Focus on your breath and bring to mind the people, experiences, and blessings you are grateful for. Feel the warmth of gratitude filling your heart.

Thank-You Notes: Write thank-you notes or messages of appreciation to friends, family members, or colleagues. Let them know how much you value their presence or kindness in your life.

Visualizations

The Dream Home Visualization: Close your eyes and imagine your dream home in vivid detail. Picture the architecture, the surroundings, and every room's interior. Feel the emotions of living in this space—the comfort, joy, and fulfillment. Take a mental tour, exploring every corner and space. This exercise can help clarify your aspirations and motivate you to work toward them.

Career Success Visualization: Envision yourself at the peak of your career success. Imagine the position you've achieved, the responsibilities you hold, and the impact you make. Visualize your daily tasks and interactions with colleagues. Feel the sense of accomplishment, recognition, and fulfillment. This exercise can inspire you to set and achieve ambitious career goals.

Health and Wellness Visualization: Create a mental image of yourself in perfect health and wellness. See yourself engaging in physical activities you love, maintaining a balanced diet, and radiating vitality. Feel the energy and vibrancy in your body. This visualization can motivate you to prioritize your health and make positive lifestyle choices.

The Goal Achievement Visualization: Choose a specific goal you want to achieve and visualize its successful accomplishment. See yourself taking the necessary steps, overcoming obstacles, and celebrating your achievement. Feel the satisfaction and pride of reaching your goal. This visualization can provide clarity and motivation for pursuing your ambitions.

Inner Peace and Relaxation Visualization: Immerse yourself in a visualization of inner peace and relaxation. Picture a serene natural setting, like a tranquil beach or a forest. Feel the soothing sensations of calmness and tranquility. This exercise can help you manage stress and find moments of inner peace in your daily life.

The Ideal Day Visualization: Visualize your ideal day from start to finish. Imagine your morning routine, work or activities, interactions with loved ones, and leisure time. Feel the joy and contentment of living this ideal day. This exercise can inspire you to structure your days in alignment with your aspirations.

Gratitude and Abundance Visualization: Create a mental image of an abundant life filled with blessings. Visualize all the things you are grateful for—people, experiences, achievements, and opportunities. Feel the immense gratitude and joy in your heart. This visualization can deepen your sense of appreciation and positivity.

The Financial Abundance Visualization: Visualize yourself in a state of financial abundance and security. See your bank accounts thriving, investments growing, and financial worries dissipating. Feel the freedom and peace of mind that financial abundance brings. This exercise can help you set clear financial goals and take steps to achieve them.

The Relationship Harmony Visualization: Imagine your relationships filled with love, understanding, and harmony. Picture yourself communicating openly and lovingly with your partner, family, and friends. Feel the warmth and connection in your interactions. This can inspire you to nurture and strengthen your relationships.

The Personal Growth Visualization: Envision your personal growth journey. See yourself acquiring new skills, gaining knowledge, and expanding your horizons.

I-Statements: Use "I" statements to express your feelings and needs assertively. For example, say, "I feel frustrated when..." instead of "You always..."

Empathy Practice: Make a conscious effort to put yourself in the other person's shoes, acknowledging their feelings and experiences with empathy.

Conflict Resolution Skills: Develop conflict resolution skills such as problem-solving, compromise, and staying calm during disagreements to maintain harmony.

Non-Verbal Awareness: Pay attention to your body language, tone of voice, and facial expressions to ensure they convey warmth, respect, and positivity.

Random Acts of Kindness: Regularly perform small acts of kindness for your loved ones to create a positive, nurturing environment within your relationships.

Setting Boundaries: Establish healthy boundaries to maintain a sense of self while fostering positive connections with others.

Active Problem-Solving: Approach relationship challenges as problems to be solved together, encouraging collaboration and mutual growth.

Express Appreciation: Frequently express your appreciation and gratitude to those you care about, reinforcing positive feelings in your relationships.

Forgiveness: Practice forgiveness, both for yourself and others, to release negativity and promote healing within your relationships.

The SMART Framework System

Specific: Your goals should be clear and precise, leaving no room for ambiguity. Clearly state what you want to achieve, who is involved, what resources are required, and where it will happen.

Measurable: Your goals should be quantifiable, allowing you to track progress and determine when you've successfully achieved them. Ask yourself questions like: How will I measure progress? How will I know when the goal is achieved?

Achievable: Ensure that your goals are realistic and attainable. While it's important to set ambitious objectives, they should still be within the realm of possibility. Consider your current resources, skills, and constraints.

Relevant: Goals should align with your broader objectives and be relevant to your life or aspirations. Ensure that pursuing these goals makes sense in the context of your values and long-term vision.

Time-Bound: Set a specific time frame for achieving your goals. Establishing deadlines creates a sense of urgency and helps you stay focused and accountable. Ask yourself: When do I want to achieve this goal?

Made in United States
North Haven, CT
25 September 2023

41947396R00085